Your Purpose
MATTERS !

Endorsements

"Davin's expertise and passion for purpose jump off the pages of this book and leap into our souls. It's a must-read!"

—**Jon Gordon**, seventeen-time bestselling author

"Davin Salvagno's *Thieves of Purpose* is a profound guide to overcoming the mindsets that hold us back. With heartfelt stories and actionable insights, Davin challenges us to confront the thieves that rob us of our potential and to embrace purpose in our daily lives.

This book is a call to action for leaders and individuals alike to step boldly into who we are meant to be and the impact we are meant to make. It's a must-read for anyone committed to living and leading with intention."

—**Garry Ridge**, chairman emeritus and former CEO of WD-40 Company

Books by the Author

Finding Purpose at Work (2020)

THIEVES
OF
PURPOSE

Books by the Author

Finding Purpose at Work (2020)

THIEVES OF PURPOSE

OVERCOMING THE 12 MINDSETS
ROBBING YOU OF YOUR POTENTIAL

DAVIN SALVAGNO

mango

PUBLISHING

MIAMI

For permission requests, please contact the publisher at:
Mango Publishing Group
5966 South Dixie Highway, Suite 300
Miami, FL 33143
info@mango.bz

For special orders, quantity sales, course adoptions and corporate sales, please
email the publisher at sales@mango.bz. For trade and wholesale sales, please
contact Ingram Publisher Services at customer.service@ingramcontent.com or
+1.800.509.4887.

Thieves of Purpose: Overcoming the 12 Mindsets Robbing You of Your Potential

Library of Congress Cataloging-in-Publication number: 2024947361
ISBN: (hardcover) 978-1-68481-827-3, (paperbck) 978-1-68481-678-1,
(ebook) 978-1-68481-679-8
BISAC category code: BUS046000, BUSINESS & ECONOMICS / Motivational

Table of Contents

INTRODUCTION

I was deeply challenged in writing this book. Countless times, I closed my laptop and told myself this topic is too hard to tackle. Like you, I have struggled with, and continue to struggle with, many of the words covered in the upcoming chapters. It almost feels hypocritical to write such a work, considering I haven't discovered all of the answers to overcoming these words. After all, doesn't the saying "he or she wrote the book on that" insinuate that the author is a subject-matter expert on that topic? Yet it is exactly why I needed to write this book. Thoughts, mental struggles, and limiting beliefs like that prevent us from stepping into the fullness of our potential and purpose. A place of struggle is not a place that one might think to discover purpose, but many authors and speakers write and speak from within their pain, from the thing bothering them most about life. Ask any artist, song composer, author, or speaker about the inspiration behind their work, and they will almost certainly tell you a story about a personal or a past struggle that they had to overcome or something they see wrong in the world that they want to make right. Our purpose can be found in our deepest struggles.

I was recently on a Zoom call with a friend whom I admitted to that I wanted to give up on this work. He is a direct person, matter-of-fact, but also sincere, authentic, and genuine. We were in the middle of a serious conversation about this book, when I shared with him my struggle. I was completely taken aback by what happened next. He paused, took off his glasses, looked down, sighed, and said, "Davin, I never planned to be a father. I don't know how to be a father. I wanted to travel, write, speak, and drive around in a really expensive car in Europe. But I met a girl, she was hot, we got married, and now we have three boys. I love them dearly, but I haven't figured out my purpose as a father. I need you to write this book so that I can discover that."

Purpose has become one of the most over-utilized words in the human language over the past decade. Yet despite how much it is talked about, few people take the time to understand their purpose, and perhaps more importantly, what is getting in the way of them living it out. This is not a new concept; questions like "What is the meaning of life?" or "Why am I here?" have been plaguing humanity for thousands of years, dating back to the ancient Greeks. The truth is we are constantly looking for purpose, whether or not we are aware of it. What we fail to recognize are the things that hold us back from realizing and fulfilling it. Purpose as a singular grandiose idea for our lives can be overwhelming, which is why few choose to attempt embarking on a discovery process of meaning and fulfillment in their lives, and many avoid the conversation altogether. Purpose, however, is not singular; it is plural. It is also not a past or future tense concept; it is present.

When we understand that our purpose can show up in multiple ways, moment by moment, and we recognize the things that can derail us from stepping fully into those moments, we can take control of our lives, unleash our potential, and experience the fulfillment of who we were created to be.

This book is a guide to doing that. Each of the words in the chapters ahead specifically call out what derails us from fulfilling our purpose, moment by moment. My aim is to challenge you to think about how you show up in these moments. In each chapter I will share several real-life examples and stories, as well as thought-provoking questions to help you identify a potential purpose obstacle that you may be dealing with, along with thoughts to help you overcome them.

Like me, even after reading and thinking through these words, you will probably continue to struggle with them. This struggle is an inevitable, never-ending part of life. I hope after reading this work, you will be better equipped for the battle in your mind when the thief strikes, that you will recognize the self-inflicted attacks preventing you from realizing your potential, and that you will glean insights that will help you fight valiantly to overcome them and step into the fullness of your purpose every day.

A word of caution: this is not a "feel-good" book. Purpose is not fluff; it is foundational. Purpose is hard and identifying it and living it out will challenge you to your core. You will need to challenge yourself in ways you have not challenged yourself before. You will need to be vulnerable; you will need to be honest with yourself and allow others to be honest with you. You will need to have conviction and perhaps most important, you will need to be forgiving. You must let go of the self-limiting beliefs of who you have been to step into the fullness of who you can be.

The friend I mentioned earlier in this introduction is my literary agent, Scott Miller, and I sent him a message while writing this asking if I could include and share his struggle of fatherhood with you. Without hesitation, he agreed. I wanted to keep his name anonymous because I wanted to be sensitive to his three sons, should they ever read this. His response: "Write whatever you want. Trust me, they know." I love his vulnerability, and I think he has a better hold on his purpose as a father than he believes.

Vulnerability, honesty, and conviction are critical keys to unlocking the best version of ourselves. They free us from the chains that bind us; they silence the lies we tell ourselves; they open our eyes to the truth about ourselves, and they direct us to whom we are meant to become.

You may have heard it said before that "the truth shall set you free." I personally have found that statement to be a profound truth in my life, and there will be a lot of truths that I share from my life that you read in this work each of us has a source of truth that we draw from—for me it is the scriptures of the Bible; for you it may be something else. Throughout this work, I will reference some scriptures that have guided me as a source of truth in my journey of purpose. The statement I just referenced, "The truth shall set you free," comes from the book of John, chapter 8, verse 32. While this book is not intended to be a religious work, it is impossible to talk about a foundational topic of life, such as purpose, without drawing from a source of truth. Whatever that source may be for you, I believe you will find the principles within this book applicable all the same.

A word on how to approach this book. Each chapter is its own thief, with some containing a related thief that could have been its own chapter. You may resonate or struggle with one of these, some of them, or like me at one point or another, with all of them. It can be tempting to jump directly to a chapter that you resonate with, but the interesting thing about the thieves is that many of them overlap and relate to each other.

Because they are so interconnected, I intentionally ordered the chapters in such a way that they flow into one another and often make references to previous chapters that you might miss if you skip ahead.

I will also note that you might find that you don't struggle with a particular thief, but I am certain you know someone who does. So, I implore you not just to read this book for yourself but also for others in your life whom you can potentially help or impact.

It can be hard to share our struggles, but they are the essence of our stories. It is in the struggle that we relate with one another, where we connect with our humanity, and where we find our purpose.
It is my hope that in sharing my stories in the pages ahead, filled with both struggle and victory, the insights and learning moments that I have gleaned from them will help you to battle the Thieves of Purpose when they come to rob you of your purpose, potential, and impact in this one life you get to live.

In Charles Dickens' timeless book *A Christmas Carol,* one of my favorite stories, Ebenezer Scrooge was visited by three spirits that transformed his life. I invite you on a similar journey. In the same way Scrooge was visited by the ghosts of Christmas past, present, and future, you are about to be visited by the Twelve Thieves of Purpose.

Are you ready?

Let's begin.

Thief #1
COMPARISON

"Comparison is the thief of joy."

—Theodore Roosevelt

I looked everywhere. Amy had just left the house to head to a photoshoot on an incredibly beautiful fall day, our kiddos, Vera and Bennett, wer playing with their friends in the yard, and Brinkley, our golden retriever, was sitting at my feet, and I was in a panic. I had spent months writing what I thought would be this very book you are reading now. I had just sat down on our couch to add a few thoughts to this work, and I couldn't find it. I searched folder after folder, file after file, I exhausted every resource, having our company's tech team look at my laptop, running up to the Genius Bar, and hours of searching blog articles hoping there was something we had missed, but to no avail. Fifteen chapters of stories and thoughts—gone. And so, I sit here typing these very words, with nothing left but pages of notes from the past year, coming painfully face-to-face with the reality that I have to start over. Yet as I process my thoughts and feelings at this moment, there is an indescribable peace within me, as I cannot help but say to myself, "How fitting, considering the title of this book."

How often do we look at circumstances and events in our life and ask, "Why?" "Why is this happening?" or "Why did that have to happen?" It is amazing that the moment things don't go as we expect or worse, tragedy strikes, our initial reaction is to question what has taken place and search for some sense of purpose or meaning to comfort our disappointment or loss. Even now as I sit here frustrated by the loss of months of work, looking for the words to describe what has taken place, I find myself looking for some sort of justification. Common phrases such as "Everything happens for a reason" or "It could have been worse" quickly come to mind. I do believe everything happens for a reason, even if we don't understand it in the moment. Perhaps I was supposed to start over, even if to include this story. Perhaps the timing of the book was meant to be later than what I had planned, or perhaps the words I had chosen in the original manuscript were not good enough, and they needed to be discarded to write something greater.

Recently, I traveled to the University of Notre Dame with our team from PurposePoint in preparation for Purpose Summit 2022. This would be the third conference of its kind that we had planned, and the largest to date. While there we learned about the deep history and divine beginning story of this breathtaking place. I was surprised to learn that the original university had burned to the ground in a tragic fire, and they rebuilt it into the renowned campus it is today.

Father Sorin, who had founded the school, after looking over the destruction of his life's work, stood at the altar steps of the only building left and spoke to the community in a moment of absolute faith, confidence, and resolution.

"If it were *all* gone, I should not give up! I came here as a young man and dreamed of building a great university in honor of Our Lady," he told them. "But I built it too small, and she had to burn it to the ground to make the point. So, tomorrow, as soon as the bricks cool, we will rebuild it, bigger and better than ever."

The university reopened four months later.

"If it were *all* gone, I should not give up!" Are you kidding me? I
could not have been given more specific words as inspiration to
rewrite this book.

When I shared the news of my lost manuscript with a friend, he said,
"What a tragedy!" While I appreciate his sentiment, and the pain
of the moment could lend itself to that description, to use such a
word to describe the lost pages of work that can be rewritten seems
unfair in comparison to those who have lost so much more that
cannot be replaced.

Take, for example, the story of Horatio Spafford, a successful lawyer
and businessman in Chicago with a lovely family—a wife, Anna,
and five children. However, they were not strangers to tears and
tragedy. Their young son died from pneumonia in 1871, and in that
same year, much of their business was lost in the Great Chicago
Fire. However, much like the story of Notre Dame, he would rebuild,
and his business would flourish once more.

On November 21, 1873, the French ocean liner *Ville du Havre* was
crossing the Atlantic from the US to Europe with 313 passengers
on board. Among the passengers were Mrs. Spafford and their
four daughters. Although Mr. Spafford had planned to go with his
family, he found it necessary to stay in Chicago to help solve an
unexpected business problem. He told his wife he would join her
and their children in Europe a few days later. His plan was to take
another ship.

About four days into the crossing of the Atlantic, the *Ville du
Harve* collided with a powerful, iron-hulled Scottish ship, the *Loch
Earn*. Suddenly, all of those on board were in grave danger. Anna
hurriedly brought her four children to the deck. She knelt there
with Annie, Margaret Lee, Bessie, and Tanetta and prayed that
God would spare them if that could be His will, or to make them

willing to endure whatever awaited them. Within approximately twelve minutes, the *Ville du Harve* slipped beneath the dark waters of the Atlantic, carrying with it 226 passengers, including the four Spafford children.

A sailor, rowing a small boat over the spot where the ship went down, spotted a woman floating on a piece of the wreckage. It was Anna, still alive. He pulled her into the boat and they were picked up by another large vessel which, nine days later, landed them in Cardiff, Wales. From there she wired her husband a message which began, "Saved alone, what shall I do?" Mr. Spafford later framed the telegram and placed it in his office.

Another of the ship's survivors, Pastor Weiss, later recalled Anna saying, "God gave me four daughters. Now they have been taken from me. Someday I will understand why."

Mr. Spafford booked a passage on the next available ship and left to join his grieving wife. With the ship about four days out, the captain called Spafford to his cabin and told him they were over the place where his children went down. According to Bertha Spafford Vester, a daughter born after the tragedy, Spafford wrote "It Is Well with My Soul" while on this journey.

Since then, "It is well" has become a foundational phrase of hymns sung in countless churches, and an anthem of hope for those who cannot make sense of purpose in the midst of tragedy, for more than a century.

We may never know the answer to why tragic things happen during our lifetime, but purpose outlives us. Even our tragedies can be used for a purpose that impacts lives long after we are gone. Spafford's story and perspective, while still uncomprehensible to me, is immensely powerful all the same. I have learned that how we respond to loss often defines the purpose of that loss, even if we are not around to see it. My intention was not to start this book off with such a grim story; in fact, I thought about taking it out. But I felt it necessary to illustrate early exactly how having such a story as a reference point in our hearts and minds can help us challenge the thieves when they attack. This book, while it may be listed under the self-help category, is not meant to be a feel-good book. It is meant to both challenge and transform both your heart and your mind. The thieves we will discuss in the chapters ahead are after both, and they are relentless.

Perhaps the most relentless thief is comparison. I have not met a person on the planet who doesn't compare themselves to others, and for good reason, we live in a society that perpetuates comparison at every turn. From social media and magazines to commercial ads and perhaps even the car sitting in your neighbor's driveway, it is almost impossible not to find a potential trigger of comparison in front of our eyes.

One of my favorite quotes used to be, "Comparison is the thief of joy," attributed to Theodore Roosevelt. In fact, that was the original name of this chapter, and I remember struggling with it as I pondered deeply about it. "Is comparison really the thief of joy?" Well, that all depends on who and what you are comparing yourself or your situation to.

As a society, there few things we do more than compare ourselves, and our lives, to the lives of others. Often, we do so with a focus on how others have it better than we do. It's easy to look at the lives that others are living—their successes, their accomplishments, their accolades—and suddenly find ourselves steeped in envy. The grass is always greener on the other side, or so it would seem. The reality is, some are battling the most unimaginable of circumstances that this life can deal us, and yet we rarely compare our lives to those stories. If we even dare to do so, we might find ourselves filled with sympathy, perhaps empathy, sometimes with gratitude, and sadly even with pity. The truth is that compassion can lead to a whole host of emotions and feelings, both positive and negative. Of those feelings, I have found that empathy and gratitude are often bridges that lead us back to purpose when we get lost in the comparison game.

> *"Empathy and gratitude are often bridges that lead us back to purpose when we get lost in the comparison game."*

I shared these thoughts with a high school business leadership class that I once taught at Oakland Christian School in Auburn Hills, Michigan. I put up Theodore Roosevelt's quote on the screen: "Comparison is the thief of joy." This ignited an insightful debate. On one hand, comparison can be a positive thing. It can cause us to count our blessings, it can cause us to compare our current selves with our past selves and convince us to return to a past better version of ourselves, or it can give us a glimpse of what is possible, motivating us to become the best possible version of ourselves. However, this is not the comparison game that we often play in our minds. We tend to compare ourselves to others, to their blessings, to their accomplishments, to their picture-perfect lives, which can be demotivating, dangerous, and destructive.

So how do we know when comparison is helping us to fulfill our purpose versus robbing us of it? Easton, one of my students in the back of the class, raised his hand during our debate so fast that I thought his shoulder had popped out and made this profound statement: "Perhaps, comparison is not the thief of joy; envy is." What a tremendous moment of insight—comparison in the form of envy is the thief of joy.

Therefore, I would offer this: If you have lost your sense of joy through envy, it is that type of comparison that it is robbing you of your purpose, since joy is often the evidence of purpose being present in our lives.

An article I recently read in *Psychology Today* states it this way:

"People generally engage in either upward or downward comparisons. In upward comparisons, we compare ourselves with those we believe are better than us in some way; in downward comparisons, we do the opposite. When we just want to feel better about ourselves, we tend to engage in comparisons to people worse off than we are. When we want to improve, we may compare ourselves to people roughly similar to us but higher achieving in one trait or another."

I have often found myself comparing myself to roughly similar but higher-achieving people, especially in the competencies of writing and speaking. And while the article I just referenced suggests that it may be out of a desire to improve, it can also become demotivating and crippling.

Ever since I wrote my first book, *Finding Purpose at Work*, I have struggled, and I've felt guilty about that struggle.

The day your physical book shows up in a box on your doorstep is supposed to be a joyous and memorable moment as an author. However, for me, in what should have been a moment of rejoicing, gratitude, and completion, I was overcome with regret, jealousy, and comparison.

"Why was my book formatted this way? It's thin and flimsy, it's not at all what I expected!"

"Look at these others" (as I glanced at my bookshelf), "they are solid and better structured. No one is going to take this work seriously.

I should have written more. Maybe I should pull it, add more and republish a second edition? Maybe I should get a second book at out as soon as possible so I am not discounted as an author?"

In comparison with the stories of deep tragedy I just shared, I realize how ridiculously insignificant these questions are. Yet, despite unspeakable tragedies that occur all around us every day, it is thoughts like these that we give our attention to and that ultimately rob us of our purpose in everyday moments.

My wife, Amy, has always been a gift of grace to me, so much so that her name has been Grace in my cell phone since I met her. She often gives me more grace than I give myself, especially when it comes to the self-limiting conversations that I verbalize to her that are going on in my head.

As I was sharing my defeating thoughts about the book with her one evening, she said, "Will you stop? Look at what is right in front of you." I knew where she was going with this. She continued, "What is sitting right there?" as she pointed to what was lying on top of our shared desk in our home office.

I said, "My book."

She said, "A book, with your name on it, and a foreword by Ken Blanchard." She was referring to someone whom I had spent twenty years learning from and many years speaking about.

I said, "You are right; the thief cornered me in a moment of weakness and tried to steal my joy. Thank you for keeping me grounded."

We need people in our lives who will keep us grounded, who will help us guard against the negative self-talk in our heads. You would think that I had learned my lesson from this moment, but not so much. The next morning I walked into the office, somewhat excited to give my first signed copies to colleagues, yet in the back of my head remained the toxic whisper of the thief, reminding me of the format and size of the book. I told myself that I would not mention it, that I would remember what Amy had said to me just ten hours prior, but we are human, and the words came out. I expressed my frustration about the size of the book with my friend and colleague Adam.

He said, "Come here. I want to show you something."

He took my book and placed it on a bookshelf next to another book I was comparing it to.

He said, "What do you see?"

I said, "It's taller."

He said, "Exactly; it sticks out, and perhaps that is the purpose for the way it is."

Again, perspective.

Since that time, I've received hundreds of notes and letters reaffirming the impact that first book was supposed to have and I am honored by the thousands of people who have read it, and so many organizations who provided hundreds of copies to their teams. As I mentioned a few pages ago, the thief is relentless. It's a never-ending battle of the mind, and so I keep some of those notes visible on my shelf in my office each time a battle stirs up to remind me of the impact and purpose that book was uniquely intended for. Another helpful source of affirmation is social media and the many messages of gratitude that I receive daily, which serve as an encouraging reminder of my purpose when the thief strikes.

Social media platforms are perhaps one of the most powerful yet dangerous inventions of our time. Never have we been able to reach and connect with so many people so quickly, while also getting a glimpse into the lives that others live. There has been much research done and plenty of pieces written on the dangers of social media, so I'm not going to go into depth on those here. On the flip side of that coin, there has been much good that has come from social media, from connecting long-lost family members and childhood friends and classmates to raising awareness on a myriad of important issues, raising countless amounts of dollars to support worthy causes, and promoting events that have brought communities closer together. It's also likely that without social media you might not even be reading this book. I've estimated that roughly 90 percent of the work that I have done and the relationships that I have formed over the last ten years stemmed from social media.

Yet as powerful as a platform for good social media can be, for those who use it properly, it is also a deep breeding ground for unhealthy comparison. As we scroll through our feeds, a subtle battle begins to take place in our minds. We can choose to be mindful and take in information that is constructive, ideas that we can learn from shared by others, and act on opportunities to both celebrate and support what is happening in the lives of others through our social engagements. Or we can choose to start comparing ourselves to others and the lives they are living rather than focusing on the lives we're supposed to be living, and we get distracted from our purpose in that moment.

In addition to being a gift of grace to me, my wife, Amy, is also a talented photographer and writer. Prior to becoming an amazing mother to our two children, she majored in journalism, graduated from Western Michigan University, and worked as a journalist at several local papers until our daughter Vera was born. From the moment we brought her home, Amy was captivated by taking pictures of Vera with her professional work camera, and while Amy was not yet a professional photographer, the pictures she took were stunning. I mentioned earlier that Amy has always been the physical expression of grace to me, and so we chose Grace as Vera's middle name. So, it was only appropriate that shortly after discovering Amy's talent for taking pictures, Captured by Grace Photography was born. As great as her work was from the start, I have watched her continue to perfect her craft over the last ten years as she has shared her gift, taking pictures of hundreds of families. These pictures usually get posted on social media, and as they receive hundreds of positive engagements and comments, the thief approaches, for as I said, social media is its breeding ground. As Amy scrolls through her feed looking at the work that so many people tell her is amazing, she can't help but compare it to the work of other photographers who have been working on their craft longer. As amazing as her work is, the thief comes to criticize it and rob her of her joy and purpose as a photographer. Thankfully, she is surrounded by people whose voices overcome the degrading words of the thief, and good thing, because without those voices, the loss of joy can quickly slide into depression and a mindset of defeat, causing Amy to park her unique gift and talents on a shelf to collect dust, leaving one of her many purposes in life to go on unfulfilled.

As I shared in the introduction, and will elaborate on in a later chapter, each of us has not just one but multiple purposes. The starting point of identifying purpose is knowing what your unique gifts and talents are and aligning them with where there is an immediate need to use them. We don't get our purpose from the world; we give it to the world. Often the opportunity for us to step into our purpose is in the midst of adversity—or worse, tragedy.

"We don't get our purpose from the world;
we give it to the world."

Perhaps you are reading this and are struggling with something at this moment. If so, it is critical for you to pause and identify which question you are asking in your mind. Are you asking "why?" or "what?"

Are you asking, "Why is this happening to me?" Or are you asking, "What is it that I am supposed to learn or do in this moment?" The more that we can focus on asking "what" we are supposed to learn or do in each moment, the more we will discover opportunities to fulfill our purpose in those moments. Each day we can make a difference. However, if we are not careful, we can fail to navigate the comparison game correctly and quickly lose sight of our purpose. Discerning how comparison is showing up in our thoughts is critical.

Comparison in the form of envy is the thief of joy, and evidence of the purpose of whatever moment we are in being robbed from us.

Comparison that convicts us to be a better version of ourselves can direct us to pursue and fulfill our purpose, particularly in moments of adversity when we feel empathy for others, and a desire to step in and help.

We must recognize the difference when comparison begins to speak to us and ask ourselves, "Am I feeling envious of others, or convicted to be better for others?"

If you find yourself experiencing envy, stop and ask yourself, "What am I grateful for right now?"

If you find yourself convicted to be better, pause and ask yourself, "Who am I trying to be better for, and for what reason?"

If you find yourself experiencing empathy for someone in a challenging moment of adversity, pause and ask yourself, "How can I help?"

Purpose in its purest form is demonstrated in service to others, but the thief wants to make our purpose about ourselves. Comparison is simply a tactic the thief uses to try and do that. These simple questions and brief moments of introspection are tools that can help us keep the thief away and keep our focus on opportunities to step into our purpose in every moment.

Four Thoughts to Overcome the Thief of Comparison

1. How often do you check your mindset when you get caught up in the comparison game? Where can empathy or gratitude right now help you find your way back to purpose in the moment?

2. Who do you have in your life that knows you as good, if not better than yourself, that can keep you grounded when the thief in your head strikes? How often do you openly share your challenges and struggles with that person?

3. How can you be that person for those around you? How often do you take your focus off of yourself and what you may or may not have to focus on the felt needs of others?

4. When moments of adversity arise, are you asking, "Why is this happening to me?" Or are you asking, "What is it that I am supposed to learn or do in this moment?"

Thief #2
COMPETITION

"None of us is as smart as all of us."

—Ken Blanchard

Almost every Tuesday and Thursday for the past twenty years, I would wake up at 5:30 a.m. and drive to the Onyx ice arena near our home in Michigan to enjoy an early morning skate with a few friends. Each morning, I faced the same mental battle—stay in the comfort of my sheets or get up and skate. As much as I enjoyed playing hockey with friends, getting some good cardio in, and partaking in a good cup of coffee and conversation after, the warm sheets of my bed were far more welcoming than the cold air of Michigan that waited outside my door. Peer accountability is an amazing thing. I knew that there were friends waiting for me, and not showing up would negatively impact the balance and enjoyment of the skate. Having the right number of players on the ice, especially if we had two goalies show up, was critical for a good skate. Not having enough players or any goalies would turn our game into a glorified exercise session shooting at the posts of the net. You could say that competition is a critical component of purpose, especially when it comes to sports. If there is no opponent, there is no game.

Our game suddenly came to a stop in March 2020 when the COVID-19 pandemic hit. For the next two years, I missed my friends, missed our skates together, missed the early morning exercise, and put on a few unwanted pounds. As the world slowly returned to safety, I long waited for hockey to return, calling the ice arena every month to see when we could resume our early morning routine. In September 2022, I noticed that drop-in hockey had returned to the Onyx calendar, and I was elated! Gripped with anticipation, like a kid on Christmas morning, I packed up all my hockey gear, turned into bed early, and set my alarm. I could not wait to see my friends and for our game to resume!

Morning came and I pulled up to the Onyx ice arena with great expectations, and as I walked up to the desk to check in, I saw just one other name on the list, and I didn't recognize it. I was immediately deflated. The lyrics of "Empty Chairs and Empty Tables" from *Les Misérables* (the best musical of all time, in my opinion) started to ring through my head and a deep sadness set in. No friends, no competition, no game. The purpose for what I had planned was lost, but perhaps there was a different plan. There was one other name on the list, after all. So, after much debate with myself, I decided to suit up and head out onto the ice, and I am glad that I did. I met the other name on the list; his name was John. We skated together for an hour and ended up having an impactful discussion together, potentially a life-changing one for him! Competition was a nonfactor, and the work of purpose played on. Had I solely focused on the element of competition, I would have missed out on the intended purpose of that moment, and the potential impact on John's life through our conversation together. While a healthy level of competition can be a good thing, competition itself is often a distraction from purpose. The key to knowing the difference is where we place our focus.

Are we focusing on what we have to gain or on what we have to contribute? While competition can foster contribution, competition without contribution is purposeless. And if we focus too much on competition, we can miss out on impactful moments of collaboration. All too often we care more about who gets there first, rather than on how we can get there faster together and who gets the bigger slice of the pie rather than making more pie together.

> *"All too often we care more about who gets there first, rather than on how we can get there faster together."*

In the fall of 2020, the world was still reeling from the deep impact of COVID and many people were still working from home as offices of the majority of businesses remained closed for what had been almost a year. While for some people, and for some businesses, remote work had proven productive and beneficial, the fallout to small businesses, particularly shops and restaurants in cities that counted on consistent lunch traffic to survive, was devastating. Many initiatives were taken by federal, state, and local governments to help businesses survive this challenging time. One specific effort in my area was a local county grant to help businesses drive more traffic to them by improving their website performance and social media presence. Our team at PurposePoint had applied to receive the grant, and something struck us as we read through the application process. We realized we knew several people on our team and in our network who possessed specific skill sets that could contribute to this project and that if we brought them together, we could qualify not just as a recipient but also as a vendor of the grant to other recipients. We were not a media company at the time; we focused specifically on leadership and organizational development through speaking, coaching, consulting, and training. While we, like most in our industry, had pivoted to virtual workshops and events due to the pandemic, our revenue as an organization was still down about 80 percent, with a couple of months remaining in the year. Our traditional business was speaking, coaching, and training; it's what we loved to do, and in pre-COVID times, we got paid well to do it.

I've shared in many of my works and talks that purpose is a combination of four things: What you are good at, what the world needs, what you love to do, and what you get paid to do. It's easy for us to fall into the trap of focusing solely on doing what we love to do and getting paid for, but these are not the primary elements of purpose. Discovering our purpose individually or organizationally first begins by asking ourselves what it is that we are good at, and what the world around us needs right now.

We took a deep look at what each of us was good at, what our unique gifts, talents, and abilities were, and how we could collaborate to help others in this deep time of need. We also reached out to our network, including some organizations that many would label as competitors in our space, but we weren't focused on competition or gaining market share; we were focused on simply serving whomever we could, and serving them well. Almost overnight, PurposePoint Media was born. Over the next two months, we pulled a team together from across the country, served forty-two companies, helping each of them improve their website performance and social media presence, and in the process recovered about 50 percent of our lost revenue for the year.

Imagine if we were so focused on our individual needs, getting our slice of the pie, competing against each other rather than working with each other—the impact that could have been lost. As I said earlier, while competition can be healthy, it can often rob us of collaboration, and in essence, be the thief of the purpose we are supposed to deliver together in the moment.

I love this perspective from Hubert Holy, former CEO of Best Buy and author of *The Heart of Business*:

> The problem is the idea of being the best implies that the
> world is a zero-sum game. There is room for only ten people or

companies in the top ten. You can only become number one by knocking off someone else. And then what do you do when you become number one?

There is nowhere else to go but down. Of course, there is competition, and competition is important. But competition against oneself, or doing better tomorrow than we did yesterday, takes us further than obsessively measuring ourselves against others. We all work and lead best when we embrace vulnerability, learn from failure, and strive to be our best rather than the best. For it is in these imperfections that we can truly and deeply connect with others.

Our pursuit to be the best or to be number one, while admirable, can also cloud our view of a greater purpose beyond the accolades that come with great achievement.

Recently Amy and I started watching a show entitled *For All Mankind*. It is a unique spin on the race to space, in which the Russians are the first to land on the moon, and as a result, history dramatically changes as we know it. A few seasons in, the race continues, but this time to be the first to land on Mars, but the pursuit of this great achievement ends up coming with a much greater cost than both NASA and Russia planned. In a three-way battle to reach the red planet between NASA, Russia, and a new contestant named Helios—a privately funded space program—character is tested at the highest level as decisions are made between saving lives or winning the race. At one point, all three end up on Mars with the realization that there is not enough water to survive the length of their trip or their return home. The only way to survive is to find water on Mars, and so a new race begins. Water is indeed discovered, but rather than collaborating to get to it faster, competition takes the upper hand, and once again lives are lost in the pursuit of selfish ambition, overachieving a common purpose.

I'm saddened by how much lost opportunity I see in the world to solve some of humanity's greatest problems due the selfish ambition, pride, and ego, and no industry is immune—for-profit, nonprofit, even in the faith sector.

Consider this: two pastors walk into a coffee shop and the first pastor orders his coffee, kindly asks the barista about their day, and then says, "Tell me, do you know Jesus?" The second pastor cuts into the conversation and says, "Hey, don't talk to her about Jesus! Jesus is my thing!"

You may laugh, but this is the sad truth for many churches and religious organizations. All too often, a competitive mindset of who gets the credit, or gets there first, gets in the way of the purpose we are here to accomplish. For example, in the for-profit sector the race is currently on to produce autonomous vehicles, which reduce emissions, traffic congestion, and accidents. All noble purposes. Many automotive companies have figured out different elements of producing such a vehicle and the infrastructure to support it, but most of them are more concerned about protecting their intellectual property and patents, rather than collaborating and sharing best practices to make it a reality sooner for the sake of humanity. The statistics of what it would take to solve many of the challenges and problems across the world as basic as hunger and lack of clean water, suggest that if the world's largest organizations would simply come together to solve them, they could be solved. The challenge is people are inherently prone to competing with each other rather than collaborating.

Observe human behavior, and most of the time you will see people in a public setting grabbing the biggest slice of pizza or the largest piece of cake. I've observed this with our children for years, and even have tried to instill in them to leave the bigger or better piece for each other. A few years back, I interviewed Gabrielle Broche, author of *The Purpose Factor*, and she perhaps said it best when she said, "Everyone is so focused on getting their share of the pie, when if they just realized we have a whole kitchen, we can just choose to make more pie together."

Competitive nature is simply an inherent element of life. We once had two guinea pigs named Chickie and Flash. They affectionally became known as our pandemic pets, which we picked up during COVID to keep us company and to focus on serving together in our home. While the intention was for each of us to take turns feeding them, that task quickly fell to Amy and me as our kids would fight over whose turn it was not to feed them. The new rule became the first person to come downstairs feeds the pigs. During the week of Christmas break this past year, I was the first person downstairs each morning, and had the honor of feeding them, and each day I observed the same behavior, as I would place four celery sticks in their habitat, two for each of them. Flash would always be the first to grab one, and Chickie, rather than grabbing one of the three remaining celery sticks, would chase Flash and grab the celery right from his mouth. If Flash grabbed another celery stick, Chickie would drop the one he was eating and take the new one from Flash.

Our human behavior is not dissimilar; as I mentioned in the first chapter of comparison, we are often more concerned with what others have rather than being grateful for what we have.

According to the NeuroLeadership Institute, "When we engage in competition, our brains release a hit of dopamine that feeds our reward system. Competing, and imagining winning, causes our brain to react positively, encouraging us to continue to engage in that same behavior. That's one of the reasons why many of us enjoy competition and how it can lead to a temporary boost in performance."

Note the word *temporary*. Even the most accomplished have struggle with a lost sense of purpose when competing is done.

Michael Phelps, the most decorated Olympian of all time with twenty-eight medals, struggled with deep depression when he finally retired. The fierce desire to be the best consumed him and he became inseparable from who he was as a person. Phelps shared during an interview, "I was always hungry, hungry, and I wanted more. I wanted to see what my max was." He went on to say that intensity has a price; that once he lost the desire to compete, he lost the desire to live.

Thankfully, Phelps sought help and has emerged as an advocate for those struggling with depression and has since started the Michael Phelps Foundation, which today is proactively helping countless kids and families safely navigate the competitive waters of life.

Research on the relationship between competition and performance is mixed; there is evidence that the costs and benefits of competition differ between individuals. Intense competitive pressure can cause us to lose sight of a greater purpose for our lives, and for many organizations, it is the cause of "mission drift," a term coined by author Peter Greer, who aptly describes the negative implications of an organization who departs from its founding purpose under the pressures of performance.

Fortunately, competition isn't the only thing that lights up the reward centers of the brain or that results in increased performance. In fact, while there are rewarding aspects of competition, collaboration is more rewarding because of the positive social feedback that comes from collaborating with others. Teamwork and collaboration lean into our strong desires for social connections, creating a similar and—I would offer more powerful— response. The benefits of collaboration far outweigh the downsides, and while competition can result in a quick surge of performance, collaboration sustains it.

 "While competition can result in a quick surge of performance, collaboration sustains it."

One of my favorite movies to watch when we were young parents was *Monsters, Inc.* How could you not love a movie with Billy Crystal and John Goodman? As entertaining as they are, more impactful than their iconic acting and comedy, is the tremendous lesson that this film portrayed. If you are not familiar, the premise is set in a monster world, where monsters like those played by Crystal and Goodman go to work at a scare factory each day. They are assigned doors are portals to children's bedrooms in the human world. Their mission is to quietly enter each room and create the greatest scare possible. The fear created by the screams of the children is then converted into energy, which runs the monster world. The competition to be the best in this film is fierce. In a surprise ending (spoiler alert), Billy Crystal's character accidentally makes a child laugh, and the monsters discover that laughter is ten times more powerful than fear!

This is the image I would offer you between competition and comparison. Competition, like fear, can be powerful, and, in some ways, healthy. But in every circumstance, collaboration is much more powerful and far healthier.

As I just typed those words, I initially wrote, "In almost every circumstance, collaboration is much more powerful." But I intentionally changed that sentence to "every circumstance" and included this note to challenge you. Can you think of an instance in which collaboration would not yield a positive outcome?

One of my favorite phrases has always been culture eats strategy for breakfast, made famous by the legendary Peter Drucker.

Everyone who has heard that quote, and experienced a great
culture, knows it to be true, and yet still far too many leaders
prioritize strategy over culture, and wonder why their organizations
struggle to achieve their purpose.

Similarly, I would offer collaboration eats competition for breakfast.
There is no shortage of articles written on the healthy culture
dynamics and organizational benefits of collaboration. I recently
read a piece in *Forbes* written by Shawn Kent Hayashi who
captures this so well. She offers:

> If you want to create a culture that will produce breakthrough
> results, collaboration trumps competition by a long shot. You
> want people to understand what their individual strengths are
> so they can pool those strengths and move toward a common
> vision. Once collaboration is in place, people are much more
> trusting of each other, more willing to stretch themselves and
> more likely to create amazing results.

> The opposite happens when competition starts showing
> up. People hoard systems, information, and support staff.
> They're less likely to share all kinds of resources—physical and
> intellectual. Those who see solutions for problems don't share
> them until they can be sure they'll get the credit. It's impossible
> to get to the best ideas when people refuse to share and work
> through thinking together.

> When competition is in play, people don't trust each other
> enough to authentically create stretch goals that will enable
> everyone to grow beyond where they are now. If you sincerely
> want a group of people to be high-performing together,
> you don't want to create a culture of internal competition
> within the team.

So how do we shift our innate tendency to be competitive to become more collaborative? The first thing we need to do is to genuinely and authentically want to. I can provide you with all the case studies in the world to prove that collaboration offers much more than competition ever will, but even then, you might only want to make that change because of how doing so might benefit you. But this first step has to come from within you; it has to be rooted in a desire to not gain from making such a change, but contributing to someone, or something—a purpose outside of yourself, a genuine desire to make a difference in the lives of those you interact with every day. It requires you to replace your programmed inward mindset with an outward mindset.

In its bestselling book *Outward Mindset*, The Arbinger Institute compares these two mindsets: "An inward mindset is a way of seeing ourselves and others that keeps us focused on our own needs, wants, and goals, often at the expense of others."

When we live and work with an inward mindset, we see people as objects rather than as people, as a means to a selfish end, rather than as individuals with their own thoughts and feelings, whom we can both learn from and impact. In my work, I have found this to be the root cause of every poor workplace culture I have come across. It is this mindset that has perpetuated a significant majority of people to be "actively disengaged" as Gallop measures in their annual workplace surveys. No one wants to be seen as an object to be used but rather as a resource to be valued. Early in my career I thought that's what human resources meant, and while I hope for one day that to be true, the reality is that in many organizations it is not.

My challenge to many business leaders today is to rethink their purpose and reprioritize their resources. If you are a business leader and you are reading this, I ask you, are you using your people to build your business, or are you using your business to build your people?

Which is the purpose, and which is the resource? Some of the most impactful and healthy organizations I have come across are clear: people are their purpose, and the business is the resource. Business leaders who focus on building their people will find their people building their businesses. This is the power of an outward mindset.

But no matter the staggering amount of evidence that is out there to support my claim, many leaders still get this wrong, and they try to justify it, which makes it worse.

The Arbinger Institute offers: "When we choose to see people as objects, we look for ways to justify this choice and become invested in seeing them as less than ourselves, which invites them to respond poorly to us in return. Until we can escape this need for justification, we will continue to wallow in the problems that are to a large degree of our making. Until we can learn to acknowledge the obvious truth—that our coworkers, family members, and neighbors are as important and legitimate as we are—then our relationships will continue to be strained and the results we accomplish together much less than they could be."

This world would be a much better place, with many of humanity's greatest challenges solved, if more people would simply adopt an outward, collaborative mindset instead of an inward competitive mindset. But as my dear friend Garry Ridge, former Chairman and CEO of WD-40 Company who built one of the most engaged and collaborative cultures on the planet, often says, "This stuff is simple, but it's not easy."

Most of the changes we need to make in our lives to become better versions of ourselves are simple, but not easy, which is why most people quit as quickly as they start. The reality is that our actions hardly ever align fully with our intentions. Think about how many books you may have started but never finished, or perhaps that fitness goal or routine you set for yourself that life got "too busy" for. I put *busy* in quotes because we will cover busyness as an excuse in a later chapter. Improving ourselves may be an inside job, but it requires outside accountability. When we approach life with a collaborative, outward mindset, we will find ourselves surrounded by people who will help us stay accountable to the changes we know we need to make to become the best version of ourselves, not just for ourselves but for those around us. Purpose is not about us at all. Purpose is about our impact on those around us. Without others, our purpose has no impact, and, therefore, no meaning.

"Purpose is about our impact on those around us. Without others, our purpose has no impact, and, therefore, no meaning."

Every other Monday, I have the opportunity to spend an hour virtually with amazing peers and colleagues who are a part of the Marshal Goldsmith 100 coaches community, also known as the MG100. Every one of these coaches is an accomplished individual, filled with a wealth of knowledge, insights, and experience. It's truly an honor to be a member of this incredible group of human beings. And perhaps what makes them so special is that they embody that term, *human beings.* Often, we tend to put such people of notoriety on a level of exclusivity or unapproachability because of what they have done rather than recognizing people for who they are. What makes the MG100 community so special, is there is no spirit of competition, only one of full collaboration. Each person in this community has a genuine desire to make a difference, they have developed an outward mindset, and they embrace constructive feedback and accountability from each other. In fact, we don't even use the term *feedback* anymore; we have replaced it with "feed-forward" because when embraced and applied, feed-forward helps us move forward, becoming better versions of ourselves.

On a recent call, we discussed the topic of loneliness and how to combat it. I was astounded at how many coaches, despite being part of such a well-connected and collaborative community, admitted that they struggled with some sense of loneliness. When asked in one of our breakout sessions about my relationship with loneliness, I responded that I feel like I have the opposite problem. I have been blessed by such an incredible and extensive network of people who are passionate about purpose and making a difference in this world that it is almost a full-time job to make sure I stay genuinely connected with each of them and leave no message unanswered—a task I am still trying to master. But what emerged from that conversation was that it was the common connection to a sense of purpose outside of ourselves that my community shares; that is the reason there was not some sense of loneliness. In essence, we derived that a shared sense of purpose is the antidote to loneliness.

We were not meant to go it alone. We were created for community, for collaboration, to contribute to a purpose greater than ourselves, and to make a difference in this world through the lives of those we touch on a daily basis. Competition creates separation, isolation, and in many cases, loneliness. It robs us of the purpose we were created for.

Four Thoughts to Overcome the Thief of Competition

1. Develop an outward mindset to become more others focused and to intensify more frequent opportunities to step into your purpose. Consider reading *The Outward Mindset* by the Arbinger Institute.

2. Embrace feed-forward and accountability from others. When provided advice or even criticism, resist the urge to become defensive or to take it personally, and instead think of how what you heard can make you better or more impactful.

3. Define the specific impact you want to make in this world. We can quickly become envious of the success of others and lose sight of the impact we want to make. Be more focused on how you are impacting someone specifically than on how many people you are impacting.

4. Identify and connect with others who want to make that same kind of impact and find opportunities to share ideas, best practices, and resources to make an even greater impact together.

Four Thoughts to Overcome the
Thief of Competition

Thief #3

IMPATIENCE

*"Impatience can cause wise people
to do foolish things."*

—Janette Oke

"This is so good—I have to post this now!" I can't count how many
times I said those words in my head and rushed to share something
on social media that had I waited a few days or even a few more
hours would have had more meaning or a much greater impact. In
fact, perhaps there is not a day that goes by that I don't think about
the imperfections of my first book because of my impatience. The
truth of the matter is that I was in a rush to get the book out, not for
notoriety or self-promotion, but because we were in the middle of
the COVID pandemic and there were people who I had wanted to
make sure had the opportunity to read it to honor the impact they
made in my life.

The reality of that time was that we were all facing our mortality;
we were uncertain and overly cautious, taking unthinkable steps
to protect ourselves and our families from a new, unknown, and
seemingly deadly disease. I'll never forget the weeks on end
that I alone went to the store to fetch provisions, while my family
didn't leave our home, and returning to our garage where I would
spread groceries out on a sheet and spray them with disinfectant,
letting them sit for hours before bringing them into the house to
be washed and put away. Today that seems extreme, but at that

time no precaution seemed unreasonable. With my family confined inside our home, I retired mostly to our basement, writing feverishly to get a message out that I thought needed to be heard at the time, not knowing if those whom I wanted deeply to read that work would live to read it, and for that matter, not knowing if I would survive to even finish the work. It had seemed that no one was safe from the fatal threat of the virus. So, I wrote quickly and published what I felt was good enough. I was impatient, and the book, in my opinion, wasn't complete. The book did well but it could have done better, and my impatience in getting it finished resulted in a regret that I have carried from the day it was released. While that book has impacted thousands of people, and I have received countless notes of gratitude from many whose lives it has touched, I often think about the missed opportunity to have had that a more complete book, had I been more patient to have it traditionally published, and possibly impact even more lives.

Impatience nips at our heels at every turn of our lives to rob us of subtle moments of purpose that we are meant to deliver. It seems for me this is a daily occurrence every evening during this season of life.

When our children were ten and seven years of age, each night felt like *Groundhog Day*. Remember that 1993 comedy starring Bill Murray and Andie MacDowell? Each day Bill Murray lived the same day over and over and was constantly presented with a series of opportunities to make decisions, which he hoped would eventually end the unbearable cycle of repetition he was trapped in. If you don't know how it ends, I encourage you to go watch the movie; there are some good lessons in it to be learned.

Each night was the same routine in our house. I would usually get home around six p.m. We would eat dinner and talk about the events of each of our days. I would ask the kids if they had any homework, to which the answer was usually "no." We would clean up dinner, and then began a two-hour marathon of trying to get the kids to make their lunch for school for the next day, take showers, choose their goodnight snack, and brush their teeth, in hopes that we might have time left over to play a game or read a story together. As much as I aim to be an intentional, in-the-moment dad, the truth is that the routine exhausted me, and as a result I grew impatient. Sadly, I must admit that there were times when my impatience got the best of me, and my voice raised to levels that I am not proud of, moments that I wish I could take back.

One night, I came face-to-face with my shortcoming when I noticed our children yelling at our dog, Brinkley. They were screaming at him so loudly for not doing what they told him to do that the sound of their voices gave me a headache. In my impatience, I almost screamed back, "Stop yelling at the dog!" But then I suddenly recognized the hypocrisy of responding in such a matter.

So, I walked over to Vera and Bennett and said to them softly, "Kiddos, you don't need to scream at the dog to get him to listen. Just give him a command in a calm tone, like this, and show him what it is that you want him to do."

Their response pierced my heart. They looked up at me and said, "But Dad, you yell at us to get us to do what you want us to do."

This was a pivotal moment for me. It was then that I realized I lived my purpose at work each day, calmly and patiently listening to my team and our clients, but when it came to living out my purpose at home, my impatience got the best of me. Impatience was robbing me of fulfilling one of my most important purposes on this earth—being a dad.

Another recent pivotal moment of purpose almost also eluded me due to my impatience—being a husband. I mentioned earlier that

my bride, Amy, is a gifted photographer, though she continues to
be doubtful of her capabilities even ten years into her profession.
She, like many of us, often struggles with the thief of comparison
that I mentioned in the first chapter. Recently, I had the opportunity
to give a talk to the staff and leadership team at the Royal Park
Hotel in Rochester, Michigan. I had given talks here in the past,
for which they have generously compensated me. This time, as
we were discussing the logistics of having me back, I made a
rather unusual request. I had learned that the hotel had themed
out one of their largest suites based on the movie *Elf*, complete
with streaming paper cut snowflakes, decorated trees, and Elfish
props galore! They spared no detail, and the cost of a nightly stay
there reflected it. Each year around this time, Amy comes up with
unique backdrops for her clients to use for their family Christmas
card photos. I thought to myself that this suite would not only be
a great backdrop, but a unique experience for her clients, and one
that would differentiate her from other photographers and help her
build her confidence. So, I asked the hotel if in exchange for my talk,
we could have the suite for a day. They generously gave us two!
Amy booked several back-to-back sessions with clients over those
two days, and we enjoyed one night there as a couple and one
night there as a family. Memories were made, my bride used her
gift to serve others, and an instant air of achievement and gratitude
came over me.

But I knew what awaited Amy in the coming days. Long nights
comprised of hours upon hours of editing and no shortage of
opportunities for the enemy to get inside her head and tell her that
her work was not up to par. Sure enough, that is what happened
during her first night of editing. Instantly, my impatience welled
up within me. I started thinking to myself all the things I wanted
to say to her about what a great unique opportunity this was for
her, something that no other photographer in the area had, and
for a moment I had even ashamedly thought to myself that my
"sacrificial" barter for the suite was a waste, and that I shouldn't

have done it. But none of that was what Amy needed to hear, and I am glad that I did not allow those words to come out of my mouth.

Once again, I found myself reflecting on how often I am told that I have been given the gift of encouragement and how much I use it every day at work and became shamefully aware of how little I used it at home. Here was a perfect opportunity, a pivotal moment, to overcome my impatience, and be the encourager to my bride that my purpose called me to be, and had I been focused on myself, I would have missed it.

We think about ourselves far too often, and I believe that is likely the root of impatience. I have learned to try to catch myself to think about how others might feel as a result of what I might say, before I say it. Doing so takes patience, the opposite of impatience, which I don't always get right. But even when we don't, we have an opportunity to acknowledge our impatience and make it right, and sometimes doing just that reveals an even deeper part of our character than we may realize.

I recently gave a talk at a large real estate firm in Michigan. The firm had a couple of partners, Vito—whom I knew personally and who brought me in to coach their leadership team and advisors—and Brian—another partner who initially seemed distant. The first few interactions I had with him were brief and came across as cold. But last week, Brian sat alone at a table on his computer in the back of the room while I spoke about the difference between our actions and our intentions. I asked the group this question: "What does being better look like to you?"

Note that I asked what does it "look like to you," and not what does it "mean to you." The words we use make a big difference. I didn't want them to define what being better meant; I wanted them to envision what being a better version of themselves looked like in their mind.

Brian, without raising his hand or looking up from his screen, blurted out from the back of the room, "Being a better dad."

Surprised, and encouraged, I said, "Thank you, Brian, for sharing so vulnerably that statement. What would being a better dad look like?"

He said, "Being more patient. I am often impatient with my kids."

Without even knowing it, Brian, in a short sentence, defined how impatience was robbing him of his purpose as a father, and I related all too well. I now thought differently about Brian because he revealed his character, and I am sorry that I judged him so quickly, or even at all.

We have these thorns in our sides that seem to never go away, no matter how hard we pray or try to remove them ourselves. But perhaps they are there to keep our attention. Impatience has long been one of mine.

What I have learned is that the key to confronting impatience is not removing it; it's recognizing it. Being more aware of who I need to be in the moment, rather than what I have to get done in the moment, has helped me recognize moments where I was growing impatient.

 "The key to confronting impatience is not removing it; it's recognizing it."

That simple thought is something I constantly ask myself. Who do I need to be right now for those around me, rather than what do I need to get done? It's a trigger question for me to press pause on life in my mind to take stock of what was most important in the moment, and then to re-enter that moment with patience to focus on my purpose in the moment.

My friend Kent Chevalier, who has served for many years as the chaplain of the Pittsburgh Steelers (the other Pennsylvania football team), has a quote that I have fallen in love with: "Your purpose will always involve you, but it will never be about you."

Read that again, and this time, imagine taking a knee in a locker room with others around you, and a voice of conviction coming straight at your face, mind, and heart.

"Your purpose will always involve you, but it will never be about you."

We want things to be about us. We are conditioned to think it is all about us. But it's not. Our purpose is our contribution to others, to those around us, to the world. It's what will last when we are long gone. It will be the only evidence that we were ever here.

We also are conditioned to go, go, go. I once worked for an executive at a large Fortune 500 retailer who was famous for saying, "Speed is life." He was notorious for creating a sense of urgency to get things done, and it created an environment that made it nearly impossible for people to focus on who they needed to be and how they showed up in the moment. As a result, customer service suffered, employee engagement suffered, culture suffered, and eventually the company went into survival mode just to keep stores open. I never forgot those words: "Speed is life." Rarely does rushing anything produce a good result. I would offer that "peace is life."

In what areas of your life do you need peace? Where are you feeling rushed or pressured to get something done? I encourage you right now to take that thought captive and think about who or what is rushing you. Then ask this question: "What is the consequence of it not getting done right now?"

If the answer to that question is the difference between life or death for someone, then I encourage you to proceed with a sense of urgency, but if it is not, then I challenge you to think about the *why* behind whatever it is you are feeling rushed to do, and even more importantly, who it is for.

If it's to positively impact someone else, by meeting an urgent need, or doing something for them that is time sensitive, then I would offer that you are not experiencing impatience, but rather an invitation to step into a moment of purpose. When we take our eyes off of ourselves, and place them on the needs of others, when we involve ourselves without making it about ourselves, we prioritize what matters most in the moment.

Too often we grow impatient because we are thinking about our needs and desires instead of looking at how we can meet the needs of those around us in the moment. I am not just talking about giving of our resources, but rather our time and attention. I can't tell you how many times I have been caught in a moment not being fully present and available to someone talking to me because I was thinking about something I needed to get done. My impatience in every one of those moments robbed me of my potential purpose. Thankfully, in some of those moments I was able to catch myself, I apologized, acknowledged that I was distracted, and humbly asked the person to repeat themselves and was given a second opportunity to be who I needed to be for them at that time.

Sadly, there are other moments that I will never get back, and it's those instances that cause me to write to you now with conviction to take every moment and every thought captive and to inspire you to focus on who you need to be in the moment first, and on what you need to get done second. We often find our most important purpose when we lose ourselves in the service of others.

"Ready. Fire. Aim." I used to say this phrase quite often in my former corporate career, mockingly, as I would watch initiatives get prematurely launched due to impatient leadership, and they would often fail because we didn't take the time to aim properly before launching. Funny how we so quickly judge others without looking at ourselves in the mirror, for if we do, we might recognize that the faults we find in others, sometimes are faults of our own.

When I launched PurposePoint in 2018, I vowed that I would not make the same mistakes of poor leadership that I had encountered in my almost twenty-year corporate career. In fact, that was the reason I was launching it: to help leaders slow down and revisit their founding purpose as an organization for going into business, and their core reason personally for being in the business they were in. I wanted to challenge them to focus, not on what they were doing, or needed to do, but on who they were being, and who they were helping others become. PurposePoint started well, but as things rapidly changed over the next five years, I realized that I had become the very leader that I used to mock. What began as a one-man band quickly grew into a million-dollar company with many voices, thoughts, and ideas. I saw so much potential to keep expanding our impact, and guess what I did with every good idea? You guessed it: "Ready. Fire. Aim." It got so bad that there were moments that, before we even decided to launch an initiative or go in a certain direction, I was creating a post to announce to the world while still in the ideation meeting! It was then that my dear friend and colleague Kurt David pulled me aside and quoted this famous proverb. He said, "Davin, if you want go fast, go alone; if you want to go far, go together."

Those words stopped me in my tracks. I wanted to go fast, not because I wanted to hit or surpass certain goals, but because I wanted to see the impact. But more importantly, I wanted us to go together. As John Maxwell once said, I wanted to "do something that made a difference with people who wanted to make a difference." I realized in the pursuit of my noble aspirations, I was negatively impacting the people who had raised their hands to go on this journey with me. I had lost sight of what was important in the moment and who I needed to be in the moment, and I did not have peace. I reminded myself of the former executive who was famous for saying, "Speed is life," and I took my own medicine, "Peace is life."

Over the coming months I took time to take stock of the direction we were headed in, and with counsel, made some big decisions, which ultimately led to dissolving the company structure and partnerships that we had created, returning PurposePoint to its original form and purpose. All but two of those on our team stayed with me for what would be a new, slower-paced, but more intentional journey ahead, and with no guarantees, but I had peace, and so did they.

The road ahead was uncertain; we had pressed pause on everything, but it gave us the time we needed to rethink, strategize, and move forward together in a less stressful and more sustainable way. Even now as I write these words to you, fresh off the heels of Purpose Summit 2024, we normally would be rushing to iron out all the details for Purpose Summit 2025, largely motivated by a need to have immediate control over our circumstances, but we, or rather I, have truly learned to slow down to speed up, and I have such peace.

"Slow down to speed up" is a term I learned twenty years ago and lived by as a leader in my previous career, and it's amazing how quickly I forgot it when I found myself at the helm of a company, as small as we were. I could not be more grateful that we were so intentional early on about our purpose, mission, vision, and most importantly, our values—clearly defining them, talking about them almost every day, and using them as a regular reference point to who we, or rather I, were behaving. Had we not done that, I think that the journey would have ended, and I would have found myself looking in a mirror, all alone, asking what I had done. I have been blessed by an amazing group of people, who believed in me, who believed in each other, and who believed in the difference we can make together.

On the flip side of impatience is perfection. I would offer that perfection and impatience are two sides of the same coin, that coin being time. The key is to find the balance. This next section was originally its own chapter, but because of how closely impatience and perfection can dance together with each other, I decided to discuss perfection here as sort of a subchapter.

 "Perfection and impatience are two sides of the same coin, that coin being time. The key is to find the balance."

PERFECTION

"I am careful not to confuse excellence with perfection. Excellence,
I can reach for;
perfection is God's business."

—Michael J. Fox

We were about to introduce the Purpose Leadership Awards to our entire network with the press of a button. I looked through the email template that our marketing team put together; I then shared it with Lisa Oprita, our chief experience officer, for a lookover. Lisa normally catches everything; it is one of her many gifts and a purpose she steps into daily. We both nodded that all looked well and hit send. Within moments, we received several emails from contacts noting an error in the last sentence at the bottom of the announcement. Instead of the dates of the awards reading May 23–25, it read May 23–15. Several thoughts rushed over me in this moment. First, from an optic standpoint, this did not look professional; how could we make such a simple yet obvious mistake? Small as it was, how might this mistake damage the credibility of our organization? How do we redact and replace thousands of messages with the right dates? It was that last question that flipped my mindset.

What if we send another message, vulnerably sharing the incorrect dates in the previous email? That would give the message double exposure. People who may have missed the first email might read the second. It was reassuring to know that many people read to the bottom of the first email to find the error in the first place, which means people were interested in what we had to share.

In an instant, a flurry of negative thoughts that incited worry and anxiety were replaced by positive thoughts that infused optimism and gratitude. What was the difference? Simply how we chose to look at the mistake.

Many of us spend too much time and energy inside of our own heads focusing on imperfections that have no consequence, me being one of the many. One of my favorite places to be is on the keys as a part of our worship team at church, not because I want any recognition, but because it is the one place where I can use the gift that God gave me as a musician in harmony with other musicians using their gifts for the same purpose. Our church has never called the platform a stage—it is always a platform, and we never think of ourselves as performers but as worship leaders. That is an important distinction. The goal is not for others to see us but instead to create an environment where people can feel close to God.

I have had the honor of serving on the worship team for more than ten years, and not that I have counted, but that means that I have played in front of our congregation hundreds of times, and in every one of them I have made a mistake—hitting a wrong note or chord that most of the time only I noticed. Even though I know that many people didn't notice, for some reason, every time it happens, I have the same thought: I ruined the worship experience for everyone. The reality is that has almost never been true, but rather a distracting thought, an attack from the thief of perfection to rob me of my purpose in the moment. Sometimes I can recognize the attack and recover quickly; other times, I let it fester for hours and sometimes days.

Our worship pastor, and my dear friend Jake Sciacchitano once game me a book entitled *The Heart of the Artist* by Rory Noland. It is one of my top five books sitting on my desk with almost every page dogeared or highlighted. If you are an artist of any kind, and I would offer that we all are in one way or another, I would recommend that you read it. It does a tremendous job of helping us recognize our inner dialogue to help us understand the motives behind using each of our individual gifts. One excerpt has helped me time and time again when I find the thief of perfection attacking. It speaks of the Amish and shares how when they would make furniture, there was always a mistake or flaw in the furniture they made. They would intentionally leave the flaws in the furniture as a reminder that no one is perfect, and it is those very flaws that gave each piece of furniture its uniqueness and value.

As my dear friend Garry Ridge likes to say, "We don't have failures; we have learning moments." Like the Amish furniture, each of our learning moments makes us unique, and when we learn from them, they provide value both to ourselves and others who learn from our mistakes.

Since meeting Garry, I have learned to treat every imperfection as a learning moment, and instead of letting the mistake fester, I have marked them as reference points to be better the next time an opportunity for me to do so arises. I encourage you to do the same.

Four Thoughts to Overcome the Thieves of Impatience and Perfection

1. Recognize when you are being rushed. If you are in the presence of others, and you find yourself frustrated because they are impending something you need to get done, that is likely an invitation to pause, set aside what you need to do, and instead focus on who you need to be in that moment.

2. Don't be quick to judge others. There is little we know about each other until we make the time to learn more about each other. The more time you take to truly get to know people, the more they will reveal their character and intentions. Our impatience to take the time to get to know someone can rob us of a relationship that could become mutually beneficial, or, even better, long-time cherished.

3. Learn to slow down to speed up. This is particularly hard in a society whose pace seems to be ever-rapidly increasing. But if you do take the time to slow down, you might catch the insights and revelations that can thrust you further ahead of where you would otherwise be if you tried to keep up with the pace of society.

4. Recognize that no one is perfect, and perfection in and of itself is an endless pursuit. Learn from your mistakes to be better the next time and label them not as failures but as learning moments, and in the end know that like the Amish, even our imperfections serve a purpose.

<h1>Thief #4</h1>

DISTRACTION

"Distraction robs us of the ability to both live in the moment and discern what lasts."

—Bob Goff

Oh, the irony of writing this chapter. Sitting here with a fresh cup of coffee pondering where to begin on the topic of distraction, all I can think about is everything else I could be, or maybe even should be, doing right now. It is for that exact reason that I know the most important thing that I must do at this moment is to write these words.

We live in perhaps the most distracted era of humanity in history. With new technology all around us, and the power to do so many things in the palm of our hands, it is practically impossible to be bored. Which is why it drives me bonkers when our children, whom I dearly love, walk around mindlessly with the words, "Nothing to do?" Take the technology away and count the number of toys and games they have, and it's hard to fathom how they could possibly be out of things to do. Perhaps I have forgotten what it feels like to have nothing to do; I can't even remember the last time I said those words or even thought them.

The reality is we are living in a constant state of doing. We have become human doings, rather than human beings. We struggle to take the time to be. While it may be more prevalent now than ever, this struggle has been around long before technology. Socrates once said, "To be is to do." Jean-Paul Sartre offered, "To do is to be." Two contrasting statements, thousands of years apart.

 | *"We have become human doings, rather than human beings."*

It seems this tug-of-war between being and doing has gone on for quite some time. So, it's not a result of what we have access to or even what is going on around us. The truth is, our biggest distractions don't come from outside of us, but rather, from within us.

A recent article I read written by Nate Klemp, PhD, put it this way:

"We tend to think that we are distracted because of the devices in our pocket, Instagram, Facebook, text messages, phone calls, and the thousands of other notifications beckoning for our attention. But according to the research of two Harvard psychologists, the real problem isn't our chaotic environment, it's our minds."

Psychologists Matthew Killingsworth and Daniel Gilbert found that the human mind is wired for this state of continuous distraction. In a study conducted with 2,250 adults, they concluded that we spend around 47 percent of every waking hour "mind wandering," an experience that is so ordinary, so natural to us, we don't even notice it.

It's waiting at the gate for your plane and thinking about what awaits you on the other side of your flight or sitting in an Uber thinking about the emails you forgot to write earlier that morning. It's not being present in the moment and aware of who is around you. You have likely been there; I know I have.

We tend to think about distractions as an outside force, but it's not. As we can see from the research, it's a mindset—our default mindset. If we want to get focused, if we want to better manage the distractions of life, we must develop a new habit of intentionally focusing our attention on the moment. We must take every thought captive and retrain our brains to be where our feet are. We need to focus less on what need to be doing and more on who we are being.

There are opportunities for us to step into our purpose all around us. The problem is, rarely are we present or living in the moment. Sometimes our purpose is staring us right in the face and we rush by it because we are so focused on what we need to get done, rather than on who we need to be. I often wonder how many opportunities I have missed to make a difference in the lives of those around me because I was not present in the moment.

Let's go back to the moment at the airport gate. Picture where you might be sitting or standing. Take note of the people around you, perhaps even sitting or standing next to you. Perhaps there is a divine appointment waiting in this moment right here for you to connect with a perfect stranger. Maybe that connection leads to a new relationship, be it personal or professional, or perhaps it's as simple as an exchange of thoughts in small talk that creates a ripple of impact in either of your lives, and you never see each other again. Either way, there is a purpose for the present moment, and we often miss it because we are not present. We are too focused on what we are doing and where we are going rather than who we are being.

Let's move beyond that gate and onto the plane. I'm fairly certain you will recognize this scene. You walk onto the plane, check your boarding pass for your seat location, nod at those making eye contact with you as you casually wheel your carry-on behind you, find your aisle, politely point out your seat to those who may already be seated in your aisle, stow your bag, and take your place. Then there is the awkward silence. The game of airplane small-talk chicken begins between you and the person next to you. One of you breaks the silence with something to the effect of, "Are you heading home or is this home?" Sprinkle in some comments about the weather, and perhaps go as far as what you both do for a living. Then the conversation ends as quickly as it begins and you put in your earbuds, divert your attention to a magazine in the chair pocket in front of you, or pull out a book from your bag. You travel a few hours together in silence, and as the plane lands, the game of airplane small talk picks up with how smooth or not smooth the flight was, more comments about the weather at your place of arrival, and as you depart your aisle, a final kind gesture to enjoy whatever awaits you both as you go your separate ways.

What a tragedy. Or perhaps not. Who knows what connection or difference could have been made on that flight? Prior to the realization that any moment in time can be a missed purpose point, I can tell you, this was an all-too-common summary of many of my travels across the sky. We could get into personality dimensions and talk about the reluctance to engage in such conversation depending on your personality type, but I would offer that is not the primary issue here. While it may play a part, the larger issue is that in our minds we are focused on where we are heading and what we can get done on that flight, even if it is taking a moment for ourselves by listening to some music or cracking open a book. It's likely that on any flight we could still accomplish that, but the point that I'm making is that we often rush ahead into that next activity without being fully present in what opportunities of purpose might exist in the moment.

> *"Sometimes our purpose is staring us right in the face and we rush by it because we are so focused on what we need to get done, rather than on who we need to be."*

Those opportunities are all around us if we look and listen for them. The key is to be more focused on the people around us than the tasks before us in every moment. One of my favorite car commercials captures this so well. It portrays a little girl playing in the living room while her father is on a business call. She looks up from her toy boat and innocently asks her dad how big the ocean is. Realizing that his daughter has never seen the sea, he decides to answer her question the best way he can, by taking her there. He ends his business call and the two of them hop into their new car and they begin their journey. They drive past the tall buildings near their home, through lush green forests, and finally reach sandy shores just as the sunset casts a beautiful glow over the ocean. They take in a moment together that would have otherwise been lost if the dad were more focused on what he needed to get done rather than on who he needed to be.

I realize it's not always possible to drop what we are doing and take an impromptu road trip, but that's not the point. This is a lesson in awareness and decision-making. The dad was aware of his daughter's presence and desire to learn something. He could have easily dismissed it by saying, "Not now" or "I'm busy," as many of us often have, which I'll discuss in an upcoming chapter on excuses, but he chose to be present in that moment and prioritize who he needed to be over what he needed to get done.

I have shared that purpose is not a definitive singular idea for your life. Purpose is plural and momentary, and often we can find our multiple purposes competing for attention. My friend Dr. Amber Selling, the bestselling author of the book *Winning the Mental Game*, has an acronym she uses to help athletes focus on their most important purpose in the moment: W.I.N., which stands for "What's Important Now." When you find yourself in a moment where multiple sources are competing for your attention, ask yourself that question. What's important now? I have many purposes as a husband, father, author, speaker, business leader, worship leader, friend, the list goes on, but we can't be in two places at the same time. We have to focus on who we need to be in the moment that is most important. I'm not suggesting ignoring the other purposes but putting them in a queue and focusing on one at a time in order of importance. For me, I use something I learned a long time ago called "the vertical alignment"—God, family, business. I have found prioritizing things in that order has always served me well, even if in the middle of the chaos it didn't seem so. This is how you step into each moment of purpose, how you W.I.N. the moment as my friend Dr. Selling has challenged us to do.

We also need to recognize unproductive activities that are consuming our time, and sometimes sucking the life out of us. Mindlessly scrolling on social media is a big one. Notice I didn't say social media in and of itself. Social media can be purposeful, and I often use it to share content to positively impact the lives of others, recognize and encourage others, and be a resource to connect others to each other. But most people I observe spend an exorbitant amount of time scrolling randomly to pass the time. Ever since I have made that observation, when I find myself scrolling, I ask myself if I am spending that time purposefully. Sometimes I stop scrolling and redirect my attention to something more purposeful I need to do, and other times if I need to take a break from thinking so hard, I choose to scroll more intentionally by looking for content that I can positively comment on and reaffirm, which provides a sense of purpose knowing that I am using my gift of encouragement.

It's also been said that when we are not focused, we pick up our phone every fifteen seconds. Read that again: every fifteen seconds! I have found myself doing just that, particularly when I am waiting, whether in a line in public or simply to use the shower at home. But what if we ignored that urge? What if while in line in public instead of looking at our phones we chose to engage in conversation with those around us? What rich conversation might we uncover? What new relationships might we discover? I often think about the many missed opportunities that have passed me by because I was looking down instead of looking up. Opportunities to engage people are all around us if we are present and not distracted. What if at home I used that time to check on what my kids were doing and engage in conversation with them, maybe sit at the piano, or continue reading that book I haven't finished, things I complain that I never have time for. My eyes were opened the day they introduced the feature on our phones that showed us how we choose to spend our time. After being honest with myself, I have chosen not to allow the phrase "I never have the time to...or I don't have enough time to..." to come out of my mouth.

Another "aha" moment for me was learning how much time is lost between distractions. Studies show that if you are engaged in a task that requires mental focus, and you step away to engage in something else, it will take about fifteen minutes to get back the level of focus you were previously engaged in.

I found this to be true during COVID while working from home. While I enjoyed the flexibility to multitask, I became busy and not as productive as I would have liked. The truth is, I found my many purposes competing for my attention without the normal barriers of time and space to compartmentalize them and too many distractions around the house to easily engage in or retreat to. While working at home has its benefits, and some can manage their time diligently, I constantly asked, "What's important now?" to determine where I should direct my attention.

It might not be practical to think that we can eliminate distractions, but we can recognize and minimize them. The key to doing so is to first be aware of what you are doing, and why you are doing it. Is the time you are currently spending serving any purpose? If it is not, then whatever you are engaging in is a distraction, and you need to ask yourself how you can spend that time more purposefully.

It's also important to recognize that rest serves a purpose. We all need to recharge, and we have different ways of doing that; even

God rested on the seventh day. For some, it might be taking a nap; for others, it might be reading; yet still for some, it may be streaming or binge-watching a show. That is all well and good, as long you are actively not using that activity to avoid something else you know you should be giving your attention to in that moment. We can allow our need to "rest" to be an excuse for something we know we should do or someone we need to be. More on excuses in the next chapter.

"Discern what lasts." I love Bob Goff's quote at the beginning of this chapter: "Distraction robs us of the ability to both live in the moment and to discern what lasts." I have talked at length about living in the moment and will continue to do so throughout the rest of this book, but I want to draw your attention to the second part of that quote: "to discern what lasts."

How much time do you spend discerning what lasts? Let me ask that question more directly: how much of what you spend your time on will matter five years from now?

A wise person once said, "If it won't matter five years from now, then I try not to spend much time on it." That sentence has been a gift to me. I now constantly evaluate my time and ask myself, "Will this matter five years from now?" If the answer is no, I discern whether I am currently facing a distraction or a momentary issue that I need to minimize how much time I give it.

Time is our most valuable gift, yet we squander so much of it in this one short life that we get to live. My friend Garry Ridge always says, "Life is a gift; don't send that baby back unwrapped!" I think of how many gifts I have sent back unwrapped in life because I squandered time on distractions.

We are here for a moment; we are but a whiff in time. That time is both meant for us to enjoy and to contribute to. If you spend time on things that you are not enjoying or not contributing to, then I would offer that you are squandering the most precious gift that you have been given, one that you can never get back.

As painful as it may be, I encourage you to take stock of how you spend your time, maybe even use the feature on your phone that shows you. I hope it opens your eyes to see how much margin you truly have that you can spend more purposefully and recognize the common distractions robbing you of your purpose.

Four Thoughts to Overcome the Thief of Distraction

1. Recognize that distraction is an inside job—while distractions are all around us, we can recognize them and decide to minimize and avoid them. Don't use the easily distracted age we live in as an excuse not to focus on your purpose and achieve your full potential.

2. If you find yourself conflicted by multiple purposes, remember Dr. Amber Selking's acronym, W.I.N. Ask yourself, "What's important now?" Then prioritize your purposes in a queue and focus on them in order of importance. If it resonates with you, remember the vertical alignment: God, family, business.

3. Remember, rest is essential to life; we all need to recharge our batteries and have different ways of doing that. But rest should never be used as an excuse to avoid doing what you know you need to do, or being who you need to be, for rest, if left unmanaged and unchecked, can become a distraction itself.

4. Discern what lasts. Evaluate what you are giving your time to, particularly in moments of great stress and anxiety, and ask yourself, "Will this matter in five years?" If the answer is yes, then continue to give your time to it and see it through. If the answer is no, recognize that it might be a distraction or only a momentary issue, and minimize the amount of time you give it.

Thief #5

EXCUSES

"An excuse is a skin of a reason stuffed with a lie."

—Billy Sunday

One of the biggest life lessons I have learned came when I felt like I was at the end of my rope at the age of twenty-four. I was five figures in credit card debt and three months behind on my rent and car payments. I was working two jobs, one from six a.m. until four p.m. and another from nine p.m. until two a.m., and operating most days on just four hours of sleep. I saw no way out of my situation and was on my knees most late afternoons, praying for God to intervene somehow. One afternoon, during the middle of the week, I drove to our church after work. Our church has a large, open gathering space that we call the atrium, and in one corner is an old grand piano. This was my quiet space. I would often come here and sit with my hands on the keys, gazing out the tall windows that spanned from floor to ceiling, waiting and hoping for my prayers to be answered. If I'm being honest with myself, it was also a cry for help. Maybe someone would see me, maybe someone would recognize that I was struggling. Most days before this one, I left that space with the same thoughts that I came in with: unheard, unseen, and unhelped, but not this day.

A now good friend of mine, Kevin Reynolds, had walked into the atrium as I was about to leave. I remember him sharing kind words complementing the sounds of the notes he heard me playing, but most of all I remember him saying, "I often see you over at that piano in that corner, and have asked myself many times, *I wonder what his story is?*" I didn't know Kevin well at the time, other than he was a gifted drummer on our worship team, but I knew there was something special about this moment. Kevin and I sat down at a table near the cafe in the atrium, and I shared my story, all of it, every painful detail. And then he shared his.

While he didn't flaunt it, by the world's standards, Kevin was a highly successful person, having done well financially for himself and his family. But like Paul stated in Philippians, he knew what it was like to be in need, to have plenty, and to be content in every circumstance. In fact, there was a time when Kevin lived out of a ten-by-ten storage unit with nothing but a couch, a drum set, and a space heater. Today, Kevin owns multiple storage facilities and investment properties in several states.

I wanted desperately to know how he did it, how he dug himself out of the space he was in. I also wanted to save face; after all, I didn't want Kevin, a successful person in my eyes, to think poorly of me. So, as I shared the details of my financial struggles, I made every excuse that I could think of, and I blamed everyone for my circumstances except for myself. You could have written a Shakespearean novel with the stories I came up with. Then Kevin said something that would change the course of my life. He said, "Davin, I'll help you with your situation on one condition: don't ever make excuses or blame others for your circumstances."

Those words cut through my heart like a hot knife through butter. Kevin didn't give me money, he didn't bail me out—he gave me something more valuable: his time and wisdom. Shortly after that conversation, Kevin helped me develop a plan to get my spending under control, contact my creditors, and put a budget together that I could and did follow.

Kevin stepping into my life at that time was a pivotal moment that I will never forget, and since then I have relentlessly challenged myself not to make excuses or to blame others for my circumstances.

Too often we allow our circumstances to define us. But our circumstances don't define us; our choices do. Who we are and who we become is a product of the choices we make every day. We can choose to be the victim of our circumstances or the victor over them. We can choose make excuses, or we can choose to make a difference, but we can't make both. As my friend Scott Jeffrey Miller states repeatedly in his *Mess to Success* book series: we have to own our mess. Making excuses and blaming others makes us bitter; acknowledging reality and learning from our mistakes makes us better.

 | *"Our circumstances don't define us; our choices do."*

Those who know me know that I am a diehard Philadelphia Eagles fan, having grown up across the street from Veterans Stadium, the once-famed, now long-gone home of "The Birds," as we affectionately call them. I spent many days as a kid riding my bike up and down its concrete ramps and waited almost forty years for them to win a Super Bowl championship, which they finally did in 2018. They returned to the Super Bowl in 2023, the culmination of a record-breaking season with the most wins in franchise history, clinching the top seed in the league and the favored team to win the big game. What an incredible game it was. The top two teams in the league went toe-to-toe in an epic thriller down to the wire, tied 35–35 with just under two minutes left, when the officials called a questionable holding penalty that would give the Kansas City Chiefs the ability to kick a short field goal and run the clock down to eight seconds before The Birds could get the ball back. Eagles quarterback Jalen Hurts had put on an incredible performance, setting the record for the most rushing yards and rushing touchdowns by a QB in a Super Bowl, and there was no question that had that penalty not been called, they would have received the ball back with ample time to tie or win the game. But it was not to be. With eight seconds left, Jalen threw a Hail Mary that landed short of the end zone, and the Eagles lost 38–35.

For the next week, the questionable penalty dominated sports headlines; in fact, the Eagles received more press coverage for their loss than the Chiefs did in their win. Why? Because they didn't make excuses.

Many commentators and journalists covering the story offered that Jalen Hurts' best performance was during the press conference after the game when he said: "I think the beautiful part about it is everyone experiences different pains, everyone experiences different agonies of life, but you decide if you want to learn from it. You decide if you want that to be a teachable moment. I know I do."

Hurts was the target of many critics all season, and he constantly responded to those voices by saying, "I had a purpose before anyone had an opinion." It would have been easy for the Eagles players to blame the referees for their loss, but none did. Led by the example of their captain and star quarterback, they each owned their mess, acknowledged reality, and chose to use this failure as a learning moment. By choosing not to let an excuse rob him of his purpose, Hurts stepped into the purpose he had before anyone had an opinion, and it was bigger than a football game. He had put on a masterclass in mindset and leadership.

We all want to win. Winning inspires us and losing shapes us, but responding defines us. How many learning moments and purpose points have we missed in our lives because our natural response was to make an excuse or to blame others?

Billy Sunday's quote, "An excuse is a skin of a reason stuffed with a lie," is a line that has been such a reference point for me that I have used it to discern whether my reason for doing something or not doing something was truly honest.

It's such a powerful statement because if the reason is honest, it is legitimate. It's only when the reason is a lie that it becomes an excuse. For example, each year we get invited to many Super Bowl parties, but being the Eagles fan that I am, in 2023 we couldn't attend any of them because we hosted our own. That was a legitimate reason. But what if we weren't? What if we didn't feel like going? What if we said we had plans when we did not? That would be a lie, and thus, an excuse.

We make a lot of excuses, and perhaps none bigger than the words, "I'm busy." But if we pull back the onion, we will recognize that few of our "I'm busy" excuses hold up.

For many years I have facilitated a leadership class for the Auburn Hills Chamber of Commerce as a part of their iLead program. One year I shared this concept of getting the root cause behind the excuses and I asked the participants to take a moment to write something they knew they needed to get done but kept putting off. I asked a gentleman at the first table I called on what he wrote down, and he said, "Putting up our Christmas lights." I asked him why he hadn't put them up yet, as the next day was the first day of December, and he responded, "I'm busy." I asked why he was busy. He responded, "I have a lot of work on my plate." I asked why. He shared that his boss had just been promoted, they hadn't found a replacement yet, and he was doing both his job and his boss's. He was overwhelmed at work and had no energy left when he got home. I asked who he had told this to. "Just you guys," he said. Sitting at his table were four of his colleagues who in that moment looked at him and said, "Tell us what you need to get done today so that we take some of that workload off of your plate to help you.

You are going home early today to put up your Christmas lights for your family."

"I'm busy" is never a legitimate reason. It's an excuse, a cover-up for a deeper reason why we choose not to do something we know we should or need to do. A simple exercise of asking a series of "whys" can help us get to the real reason. This is commonly known as root-cause analysis and is a great coaching and leadership tool that I have used often not just with those I have coached or led but in my own self-talk.

"I'm busy" is probably the biggest excuse we not only say to others but that we say to ourselves. I shudder to think about how many missed opportunities that I have had in my life to be present to those who needed me in the moment because I either told them or myself that I was too busy for them. I shudder even more to think they really heard, "I'm not a priority."

Earlier we talked about the little girl who asked her dad how big the ocean was. Could you imagine if, when she asked, "Dad, how big is the ocean?" he responded to her, "You're not a priority"?

Let that sink in for a minute.

Stop saying, "I'm busy." And instead, say to yourself first, "It's not a priority."

If you feel fine saying that, then it probably isn't a priority. But if you don't feel good saying that, then that is probably conviction that whatever is calling your attention is something you need to give your time to in that moment.

 "Stop saying, "I'm busy." And instead, say to yourself first, "It's not a priority."

Another great example of this is a story you might have heard
before. A man came home from work late, tired and irritated, to find
his five-year-old son waiting for him at the door. His son asked,
"Daddy, may I ask you a question?"

His dad replied, "Yeah, sure, what is it?"

His son looked up with hope and promise in his eyes and asked,
"Daddy, how much do you make an hour?"

His dad impatiently replied, "That's none of your business. Why do
you ask such a thing?"

Hopeful, the son persisted. "I just want to know. Please tell me, how
much do you make an hour?"

The dad reluctantly replied, "If you must know, I make fifty
dollars an hour."

"Oh," the little boy replied, with his head down. He lifted his head
and said, "Daddy, may I please borrow twenty-five dollars?"

The dad was furious. "If the only reason you asked that is to borrow
some money to buy a silly toy or some other nonsense, then you
march yourself straight to your room and go to bed. Think about
why you are being so selfish. I don't work hard every day for such
childish frivolities."

The little boy quietly went to his room and shut the door.

The man sat down and got even angrier about the little boy's
questions. How dare he ask such questions only to get some
money. After about an hour, the man had calmed down and thought

maybe there was something his son needed to buy with that twenty-five dollars. He didn't ask for money often.

The man went to the little boy's room and opened the door. "Are you asleep, son?" he asked.

"No, Daddy. I'm awake," replied the boy.

"I've been thinking. Maybe I was too hard on you earlier," said the man. "It's been a long day, and I took out my aggravation on you. Here's the twenty-five dollars you asked for."

The little boy sat straight up, smiling. "Oh, thank you, Daddy!" he yelled. Then, reaching under his pillow, he pulled out some crumpled-up bills. The man saw that the boy already had money and got angry again. The little boy slowly counted out his money and then looked at his father.

"Why do you want more money if you already have some?" the father grumbled.

"Because I didn't have enough, but now I do," the little boy replied. "Daddy, I have fifty dollars now. Can I buy an hour of your time? Please come home early tomorrow. I would like to have dinner with you."

The father was crushed. He put his arms around his little son and begged for his forgiveness.

I think about the story a lot with my son. One of my favorite moments was when I was in our home office, where I am now, writing this very book, and while I was in deep thought, Bennett came up to me and said, "Dad, can you play?"

I was tempted to say, "Not now" or "In a little while" instead of "I'm busy." But I replaced both in my mind with, "It's not a priority." And what I heard was me saying to my son, "You're not a priority." I stopped, saved the last words I had written, closed my laptop, and chose to go play. In the next half hour, we built the most magnificent rainbow road racetrack out of magnets that you have ever seen. Bennett grabbed his cars from his room and for the next week raced them on that road we built together, day and night. One of my favorite memories that I will always cherish of him as a young boy is seeing him drop his bag and coat in the mudroom after school and running into the playroom to race his cars on the road we created together. Thirty minutes of my time, which led to a week-long of fun for my son, and a lifetime memory for us both.

Stop making excuses and start making memories. You can always make more money, but you can't get time back. I don't always get it right, and I regret the moments that I miss. Amy does a great job of helping me stay focused on what matters most in the moment at home, and the simple exercise of self-talk, testing the moment with "It's not a priority," has allowed me to step into more moments of purpose that otherwise would have been lost, and it can help you too.

Busyness can also breed procrastination, but at its root cause, procrastination is putting off the things we know we need to do now until a later date because we either tell ourselves we don't have time, or we just don't want to spend the time or energy on whatever we need to do.

PROCRASTINATION

Procrastination and excuses typically walk hand-in-hand, which is why I offer it here as another subchapter. More stress has been caused in my life by putting off things until the last minute that I know I could have spent time on sooner, but I told myself I didn't have time. If I'm being honest, in most of those cases, I was not motivated.

I have shared before that there is a difference between the word *purpose* and the word *why*. While they often get used interchangeably, I offer that *purpose* is your reason for being and *why* is your reason for doing. You can know what your purpose is, you can be crystal clear about it, but you can lose your motivation to do it.

 "Purpose is your reason for being and why is your reason for doing."

Take this book, for example. I started writing this book three years ago. It could easily have been done in three months. But after losing the first manuscript, I lost the motivation to write it. My purpose didn't change. It was always clear: I knew I needed to write the book; I just wasn't clear who I was writing it for. I had lost my why, my reason for doing.

Behind every why is a who, a voice inside us that tells us to get up when we don't want to. I have many whos in my life for many different things. For this book, there were many. The first is my literary agent, Scott Jeffrey Miller, whom I introduced to you in the introduction, and if you skipped that part of the book, I encourage you to go back and read it. His reason for me finishing this work had nothing to do with a publishing deal, and everything to do with him as a father. But then there were several others. In January

2024, I gave a talk entitled "Confronting the Thieves of Purpose" based on this book, but there was one problem: I didn't have time to effectively go through all twelve thieves. So, I would pick four or six to go through in-depth and share the table of contents of this work to at least identify those I did not have time to go into. I am truly grateful for anyone who comes up to me after a talk and says something that I shared impacted them, but after each of these talks, I had lines of people wanting to know more about the thieves I didn't cover and when this book was going to finally be finished. It occurred to me that I was no longer writing this book for Scott but for many people struggling with the thieves and wanting help to confront them. I had regained my why, and six months later, the manuscript was finished.

If you find yourself procrastinating on something you know you need to do, but you have lost your why, I encourage you to think about who might be positively impacted if you chose to reengage in that task or project, but more importantly, I challenge you to think about who might be negatively impacted if you don't. I think you will find that the potential loss of impact is a great motivator and will move you to action. It's easy for us to put off our goals and ambitions because the only one negatively impacted by not taking action is ourselves, and we often justify that because the pain of change is greater than the pain of remaining the same.

In fact, that is the underlying premise of this entire book. More important than anything I have to say in this work is what you choose to do with it. If all you do is read about these twelve thieves but don't take action, with each day that passes, you are being robbed of the fullness of your purpose and potential in this one life you get to live.

 "We only take action when the pain of remaining the same is greater than the pain of change."

So, I implore you, don't put off till tomorrow what you can do today. We are not promised tomorrow. Time stands still for no man or woman, and impact lost cannot be regained. Somewhere, someone is waiting for you to step into a purpose that you are either procrastinating on or making excuses to step into. Don't let the lies you tell yourself prevent you from experiencing the fulfillment of being the person you were created to be.

Four Thoughts to Overcome the Thieves of Excuses and Procrastination

1. Recognize you are a product of your choices, not your circumstances. The first step to overcoming your past is taking responsibility for the decisions in your control, learning from them and moving on, and letting go of the things not in your control.

2. Think about the reasons you have used in the past to justify your actions and test them for honesty. Were they honest? If not, identify the lie and root cause of your excuse. The next time you are tempted to make an excuse, test your honesty and ask yourself what purpose and impact might be lost if you choose to go through with the excuse you are about to make.

3. Replace "I'm busy" with "It's not a priority." Then evaluate how you feel. If you feel conviction, that is an invitation to pause and step into a purpose that is right in front of you. If you don't feel conviction, that is likely confirmation that you need to stay focused on the task at hand, and whatever is demanding your attention might be a distraction.

4. Identify when you are procrastinating and challenge yourself as to why. Think about who might be positively impacted if you chose to take action today, or, even more importantly, think about the lost impact of what might not happen if you choose to wait until tomorrow or some other day. Remind yourself who in your life is counting on you to do what you know you need to do and become who you are fully meant to be.

Thief #6

FEAR

"Fear is never a reason for quitting; it is only an excuse."

—Norman Vincent Peale

This is the longest chapter in this book, and for good reason. I believe that the greatest thief of purpose is indeed fear. It is not only the number-one excuse we use to not take action, but also the number-one excuse we use to give up on our dreams, goals, ambitions, and ultimately on the person we were created to be, the purpose we were intended to fulfill, and the life we were meant to experience.

In fall 2023, I took a road trip from our home just north of Detroit, Michigan, to Charlotte, North Carolina, for an eight-day trip of speaking engagements and meetings in preparation for the upcoming Purpose Summit being held there for the first time. If you have ever driven from the upper Midwest down through the Appalachian Mountains, then you know how beautiful a drive it is. The scenery is captivating with lush great mountains, rays of sun peeking in between them illuminating deep valleys with little nestled towns, placed like you would see them in a model train terrain. I was just about through Virginia, with about an hour and a half left in my trip when my car chimed and my gas light came on. I had lost track of my fuel gauge and quickly found myself wrestling with the grip of fear. I was in the middle of nowhere, and I couldn't remember the last time I saw an exit sign that had a gas station nearby and I thought to myself, *there has to be an exit, the gas station coming up soon.*

The next exit approached and the beautiful blue sign that usually shows logos of food and gas options came closer and closer. It was a blank. Nothing on it. I had never seen just a blue sign that read food and gas but had no logos on it, and I have taken many road trips. It almost felt like I was in a movie and this was being scripted.

I continued to drive another fifteen miles with only thirty-four miles left till empty. The next exit approached, and while there was no blue sign at this exit, I saw a gas station on my navigation screen and breathed a sigh of relief. But as the gas sign came into view, fear overcame me even more as I saw the gas station was being built—it was not complete. Have you ever had one of those moments where you thought, *Well, it's not open yet, but maybe they have some gas?* This was one of those moments.

I drove farther as the next exit approached. Still no blue sign. I pulled off to the side of the road and started searching for gas stations near me, recognizing I may need to just take the exit and look off of the highway. I had no cell reception. I began to realize that I was out of options and I was likely going to get stuck on the side of the road and have to start walking, which was not ideal since I was already cutting it close for a sponsor dinner that I was speaking at in about two hours. I gathered my thoughts and got back on the highway, praying and hoping that the next exit had a gas station, and two miles down the road, an oasis of options appeared. Gas stations and restaurants galore. I was safe after thirty-five miles of driving with a stiff neck and that burning sensation your ears get when fear has its grip on you. A half-hour of time wastefully spent in panic for no reason, time that I could have spent enjoying the scenery, and preparing my heart and mind for the sponsorship dinner.

The funny thing in all of this is that the oasis was always there. It didn't appear because I prayed or hoped that it would. The math from the moment my gas light went on would have shown that I would make it there. How might have I reacted and used that time differently had I known that the provision I needed was exactly where and when I would need it, right at the thirty-five-mile mark? I once heard it said that all fear is "false evidence appearing real" (F.E.A.R.); I love that acronym.

How many of the things that we find ourselves afraid of in life actually materialize?

How much of our time, energy, potential, and purpose is lost out of fear of scenarios that exist in our minds and are not real?

While there is a healthy form of fear, one that prevents us from danger, such as not standing to close to the edge of a cliff without proper safety equipment or pouring gasoline on a fire, most fear is irrational and holds us back from what we are meant to do and, perhaps even more importantly, who we are supposed to become. In fact, according to researchers at Penn State University, only about 8 percent of the things people worry about come true.

Matthew B. James, MA, PhD, and author and president of The Empowerment Partnership, captured this well in an article published in *Psychology Today* in 2015 entitled "Six Signs Fear Is Holding You Back," in which he wrote: "Fear is a basic human emotion. It was wired into our systems for a beneficial purpose—to signal us in times of danger and prepare us physically so we could accomplish what is necessary for survival. When warranted, fear can be one of our most vital resources. But as Helen Keller said, 'Avoiding danger is no safer in the long run than outright exposure. The fearful are caught as often as the bold.'"

He continued in his article with these observations, "We live in a climate fueled by fear. The media manipulates fear to earn higher ratings, dominating [the] majority of daily headlines. Politicians stir up fear to accumulate votes, religious leaders employ fear to keep flocks in line, and parents wield fear to keep kids from misbehaving. Fear is woven into the fabric of our lives, perhaps affecting modern adults even more than it did our caveman ancestors."

Fear sees only the downside. While nearly every choice has an upside and a downside, someone in a fearful state only identifies the worst that could happen.

Fear doesn't let you stop to think it through. Fear tells you to react immediately.

Fear tells us to avoid anything new or unknown. Whereas fear used to appear only in response to real threats to survival, now its alarm sounds whenever we stick a toe outside our "comfort zone." Fear prefers that we stay in a familiar—even if painful—situation rather than step into the unknown.

Fear constricts rather than expands who we are. Fear tells us not to smile at strangers or speak our opinions too loudly. Instead of pushing our boundaries, fear encourages us to avoid any potential failure or rejection. For example, we should not write that book, ask for that date, or apply for that promotion. If it were up to fear, we would hide in bed instead of growing into who we could be.

Fear obscures your intuition. Great decision-makers often talk about trusting their gut instincts. There's no room for that small, still voice when fear is present. All you can hear are the spiraling thoughts coursing through your mind. When you're consumed with fear, gut instincts are hard if not impossible to recognize.

Fear often keeps us from making any decision at all. A wise person once said, "Choose a path or a path will be chosen for you." Fear is the root of some people's inability to make decisions. While most individuals do not freeze in the face of any choice, fear keeps many second-guessing themselves into avoiding decisions whenever they can. Of course, no decision at all becomes a decision.

The phrase "let's hold the space" became somewhat of an inside joke amongst our team in summer 2021. We had just wrapped up the second Purpose Summit which we held in Mt. Clemens, Michigan, on the back end of a global pandemic. This was no short task. In 2021, conferences were not necessarily allowed under COVID restrictions set forth by the state of Michigan. We had spent two years planning this summit and had already canceled it in 2020. We were living in an unprecedented time of isolation, depression, and addiction, and suicide levels were skyrocketing. We knew we had to find a way to bring people safely back together, within the allotted guidelines, to reconnect them to their purpose and each other. Under the COVID restrictions of that time, theaters were allowed to hold up to three hundred people in them, schools were allowed to fill up to 25 percent classroom capacity, and outdoor events could be held up to a limit of five hundred people. So, we got creative. We utilized the old Emerald Theater in downtown Mt. Clemens and set up three hundred chairs on its main floor for general sessions. We partnered with Oakland University, who had a campus across the street, to utilize their classrooms at 25 percent capacity for breakout sessions, and we partnered with the city to close the street in between and set up a large outside wedding tent for overflow of up to five hundred people. Over the course of three days, we brought hundreds of people from across the country safely together, and the impact was positively transformational.

One group that came was the Lippert leadership team out of South Bend, Indiana, led by Dr. Amber Selking, who served at the time as their VP of leadership and culture. Amber spoke on the second evening of the summit and, following the inspirational and insightful talk, came up to me and said, "This is amazing. We have to find a way to do this in Indiana next year!"

I said, "Where in Indiana would we do it?"

And to my astonishment, she said, "How about the University of Notre Dame?"

A few moments later, Joe Colavito, an attendee of the summit that I had just met, approached me, unaware of the conversation I had just had with Amber, and said, "Davin, this is amazing. Do you know what a thin space is?"

I said, "No, Joe, what is a 'thin space'?"

He said a thin space is a place where the distance between you and the presence of God is very thin. He continued, "I have experienced two thin spaces in my life; first, several years ago when I visited the University of Notre Dame, and the second this week here at The Purpose Summit."

Joe had no idea that we were just talking about moving The Purpose Summit to Notre Dame.

After hearing Joe's words, I knew that we were being led to make that move. Going back to Dr. James's article, you could call it my gut instinct, or a nudge by the Holy Spirit, but I was certain that we were heading to South Bend. The following week we had a team meeting to discuss the pros and cons of moving the summit to Indiana. We had only held it twice, both times in Michigan, and while hundreds of attendees came from across the country, almost all of our sponsorship support was local. We knew nobody in South

Bend, except for one company, Lippert. We were suddenly gripped
with fear as a team. What if we didn't get the support we needed
in Indiana to make it work? After all, putting the summit on was a
huge financial commitment. But I kept coming back to that moment
in the theater with Amber and Joe. I knew that fear was trying to
rob us of what we were called to do. We continued to talk as a team
and concluded that if Lippert agreed to help us secure sponsorship
support, we would hold the summit in Indiana. On our next call,
they offered to do exactly that without us even having to ask. I
was now more than certain that we were heading to South Bend.
Still, one voice on our team spoke out of fear that things might not
work out and offered, "Let's hold the space"—meaning, let's not
decide just yet.

Logistically, we didn't have the time to decide, and after a team
vote, the majority agreed to pursue our gut instinct to hold
Purpose Summit 2022 at the University of Notre Dame. That
decision catapulted The Purpose Summit to a new level. Over two
hundred different companies from around the world attended,
drawing global interest in the movement we are leading and in our
organization. Even as I write these words, leaders from around the
world are making their travel plans for Purpose Summit 2023 at
Notre Dame, and plans are underway to bring The Purpose Summit
to Europe in 2025. Imagine how the impact of the summit might
have been limited if we chose to give into fear.

Overcoming the voice of fear is not easy; it's not comfortable,
and it's not going to be popular with everyone, especially those
closest to you. Our team member who voiced their concern was
well-intentioned, as will many of those closest to you when you
might need to overcome your fear, trust your gut, or step out on
faith. But purpose often requires us to live outside of our comfort
zone, and to challenge the status quo. That does not mean to be
careless or reckless; you should still use sound judgment and wise

discernment in your decisions. A best practice that I have often used is to ask myself, "What if?" That question could be positive or negative depending on how you approach it, but it has served me well in testing my gut instinct and discerning the voice of purpose over fear. Lisa Oprita, our chief experience officer at PurposePoint, often reminds us of one of her favorite quotes...

"What if I fall? But my darling, what if you fly?"

There is wisdom in this short, sweet quote. If your gut instinct is telling you that you will likely fall, then perhaps you should think twice about taking your next step. But, if your gut instinct is telling you that you will fly, and the voice of fear is holding you back, then, my friend, I encourage you to spread your wings.

 "Purpose often requires us to live outside of our comfort zone, and to challenge the status quo."

I have a dear friend, Kent Chevalier, who has served for several years as the chaplain for the Pittsburgh Steelers. I knew Ken when he was a youth pastor at our home church in Michigan fifteen years before he became an NFL chaplain. I want to share his journey, in his words, from his message, "Do It Afraid."

DO IT AFRAID

I simply want to tell you a bit of my and Erica's journey to becoming the chaplains for the Pittsburgh Steelers. Maybe it will encourage you. Erica and I were born and raised in Pittsburgh, and we met at Geneva College, and we've been in ministry together ever since we met, for almost twenty-five years. We've served all of those years together in the local church, with the last thirteen of those spent serving a great Pittsburgh church, North Way Christian Community.

It was about year ten of serving as pastor there, something changed in me. My role didn't change, my responsibilities at the church didn't change, but I began to have this feeling in my gut; I call it my "knower." I knew that God was up to something in my life, but to be honest with you, I was scared of what this meant for me and my family. I couldn't ignore it, but I was hesitant to chase it, because I was comfortable. I had it good, and I didn't want to mess that up.

Maybe you have this new idea that could change the business, but you're hesitant to pitch the idea to the owners.

Maybe you've been dating her for years now, and you know you want to be with her, but you're scared to pop the question and commit.

Maybe you know it's time for you to go public with your faith, to leverage the platform that God has given you, but you're worried about the reaction and fallout.

See, friends, I believe that there will be times in our lives when God begins to mess us up on the inside until we step into what He is calling us to do. But I have to warn you. Some of us step too soon. So, I've learned my lesson, and this time around, I waited for God's timing.

I was about two years into the frustration of waiting on God's timing when the San Francisco 49ers traded a tight end to the Pittsburgh Steelers. His name is Vance McDonald, and after the season, he and his family attended a service at North Way.

After service, Vance asked if we could grab coffee and have a conversation. That week we grabbed coffee and we talked for a few hours. There, he told me that the Steelers did not have a team chaplain at the time. He and I grabbed several coffees in that off-season, and we got to know each other.

Throughout the next Steelers season, we saw Big Ben and Vance connect on many touchdowns, but I had a different perspective about him and his wife and their precious kids. Yes, Vance was a Steelers tight end, but he was first a young husband and father. That whole season Vance would tell me how another player and sometimes he would lead the team Bible studies because there was no chaplain to do so. Off-season came, and Vance asked if I would start a discipleship group with him and a few other guys. During that discipleship journey, Vance kept saying how he wished they could have this in the Steelers' locker room. And every time he did, something would leap in my knower.

I wondered if this was the new thing God [was] going to do, but I chickened out. I wondered about my motives. Was it just to get close to these guys? I would talk it over with Erica, but I would never talk to Vance about it.

I eventually got up the courage to ask him if he was dropping hints.

I asked if he was sharing this with the group because he thought I could be the chaplain. How does one even become an NFL chaplain? He said, "I don't know, but I want to introduce you to

Coach Tomlin," to which I said to myself, "Either way this is going to be awesome."

The three of us had lunch at the Steelers facility, and we had a great conversation, which Coach Tomlin closed with, "Why don't you come to OTAs on Thursdays for the next few weeks? And then I'd like for you to speak at chapel on the last day of mini-camp."

I was pumped to see the ins and outs of Steelers practice and the facility, and the six Super Bowl trophies up close. Then came the opportunity to speak at chapel. I preached a message about Jesus, but I don't remember a thing I said because I was so nervous!

And I left the facility on the Southside with Coach Tomlin saying he'd be in touch. A day went by and I heard nothing. A few days went by, nothing. Ten days went by, still nothing. At that point I began to think that I blew it. I apparently was not the guy, so I settled back into the frustration and confusion.

Have you ever been there? Where you stepped out but there's that wait before you land? Like jumping off a dive, but before you hit the water. You begin to question your decision-making skills. *Why did I do this?* These are the moments when the thief messes with our heads. When you take that shot, when you make that move, when you make that pitch, you jump...but then you have to wait.

And in that waiting, you and I have a choice as to which voice we're going to listen to: the voice of the truth or the voice of the thief who begins to whisper the lies.

"You're not good enough to get that position. You're obviously not wanted here. You're joking to think you could ever do something like this."

The confusion I felt was mounting to a boiling point.

Three years I had been waiting, and I'm not hearing back.

Have you ever been there?

While I was waiting to hear back, I traveled to a church on the West Coast to do some training for a discipleship experience we were starting at my church, and during the training, the facilitators sent us all out for a guided prayer experience. The trainer said, "Just follow the prayer guide." And I opened up the prayer guide, and at the top was Isaiah 43:18–19. I opened my Bible and read God's words, "See, I am doing a new thing!"

And we were instructed to write our prayers...

So, here's exactly what I wrote in my journal.

God, I'm trying to discern the new that You are doing in my life.

Is it at North Way? Is it with the Steelers? Is it with both of them?

Is it something else completely different?

Either way God, I need clarity, and I lay all of this down at Your feet, anxious to know what You want for me and my family and my church family. You may have something else entirely in mind, but I can sense that You have been up to something new for a long time in my life.

I gathered up my things and stood up, and at that moment, 10:24 a.m. California time, Coach T texted, "Can you grab lunch in the next few days to talk about the position?" My hands trembled as I called Erica, and I said, "I think I'm about to become the chaplain of the Pittsburgh Steelers."

Mind you, I hadn't even been offered the position, but I just knew.

So, I went to lunch with Coach Tomlin, and he laid out his vision for the chaplain role. He said, "I'm looking for a local Pittsburgh couple who can pastor this team. I want a guy who can lead Bible studies for the players and coaches and speak and lead chapels before the games. I'm looking for his wife to lead. Bible studies for the coach's wives and players' wives or girlfriends. I want this couple to come alongside the couples on this team." I loved what I was hearing, but then he said, "This position is not hired by the Steelers, and I would like for you to consider joining the staff of Athletes in Action."

And as soon as he said it, I knew exactly what that meant.

I've known people who served with AIA, a ministry of the missions organization Cru, formerly known as Campus Crusade for Christ. I knew that people with AIA raise their full-time salary and benefits and ministry budget. And in my mind at that point, I shut it all down.

"God, you're kidding me? I have three teenage daughters."

I'm staring college right in the face. Three weddings.

"There's no way you want me to step away from a secure income and a great position to become a full-time missionary. There's gotta be another way!"

And quickly my internal reaction revealed where I placed my trust. My trust was not fully in the God I've been preaching for twenty-five years. My trust was in a paycheck, a position, in me providing for my family. I say that out loud now, and I'm embarrassed, but I don't think I'm the only one here. I'm wondering if there is anyone here who can relate.

The meeting ended with me agreeing to speak with the leadership of Athletes in Action and continuing down the chaplain search process. I was cordial, and I said all the right words, but internally I was done.

Bottom line: I was afraid. I was afraid to step out like that.

I went home to tell Erica, and we both shut it down quickly in our minds, but we didn't shut it down as far as the process.

We agreed to see it through. We agreed to fast and pray to see if this was really God.

And during that few weeks of time, we would go out on our back patio. It's our spot during the warmer months to pray and have our quiet time. And one day Erica noticed one of the ferns moving.

Here, some birds had built a nest.

We went over and the bird flew away, and we peeked inside and saw these little eggs. We would go out there and pray and read scripture and one day the eggs hatched. We could hear the little birds chirping, and we would see Mom swoop down and feed while Dad would perch himself to keep an eye out.

And as we prayed and walked down the process, God was taking us to school about what we really trusted in this life.

God began to shift our hearts to practice what we've been preaching all these years, to trust in the principle that when God guides, He will always provide, and together we decided to put our feet and our family where our mouths had been.

We took the step, with fear fighting with our faith. We agreed that together, we would do it even though we were afraid. We flew out to Colorado to meet with Athletes in Action and sign on the dotted line to become full-time missionaries. We signed the papers. We did it. We stepped out, but to be honest, we were still freaking out, even though we knew that God was calling us to do this.

Erica will tell you that she was confident [and] at the same time nervous. She was scared and stressed, so she went for a run to pray early that next morning. That's how she clears her head. And in the middle of Colorado, she said, "God, I need something to hold onto. I need you to give me a clear message to hold onto that you're in this." She came back from her run, and we went to the final worship and teaching session. And during worship, on the other side of the round stage, a painter was painting. And we couldn't see what he was painting, but when the worship time was over, the camera panned back and what do you think he painted? A picture of baby birds being fed.

Erica and I looked at each other and we both began to cry.

This was God's word to her that He heard her prayer along the side of a road in Colorado. And even though we were still afraid, we left that day confident that God was going to take care of us every step of the way.

I share our story with you today because I wonder if you have been called to you to step out into something. But you've hesitated. You've stalled. You've walked away from that dream. You've squashed the idea because it's too risky. It doesn't make logical sense. But you know in your knower that you're supposed to do it. I want to encourage you today to "Do It Afraid."

—Kent Chevalier

DOUBT

Doubt is a cousin of fear, and thus I include it here as another subchapter. Some might say that doubt is even rooted in fear, and the worst form of doubt is self-doubt. Van Gogh is attributed to have said, "If you hear a voice within you say, 'You cannot paint,' then by all means paint, and that voice will be silenced." So many paintings have been left unpainted, songs left unsung, and books left unwritten, as a result of self-doubt.

In her *Forbes* article "How To Beat Self-Doubt And Stop Selling Yourself Short," bestselling author Maggie Warrell wrote this:

"I remember being consumed by doubt when the idea of writing a book first took hold of my imagination. 'Who am I to write a book?' I thought to myself. I'd never studied writing, and I finished my education in rural Australia without ever learning where to place all the apostrophes. As much as the idea of putting my ideas into prose inspired me, I felt wholly inadequate for the task (not to mention that I had four kids under seven at the time!) It was only when my husband Andrew said, 'Why don't you give yourself permission to write an imperfect book?' that I decided to take the plunge. Was it the worst greatest piece of literary penmanship the world has ever seen? Of course not. But it's now out in the world (in six languages) and it never would have been had doubt called the shots."

I can personally relate with Maggie. I gave up on this very book many times because of self-doubt, but the fact that you are reading it right now is proof that whatever thoughts of self-doubt you are experiencing you too can also overcome. One of the remedies Maggie offers to overcome self-doubt is to doubt our doubts and recognize that they are not inherently true.

Self-doubts are your fears in disguise, trying to keep you from loss. Ironically, in most cases those doubts are keeping you back from gain, and the unrealized loss of that potential is far greater than the potential loss that may have been realized.

Your doubts are not the truth. In fact, often, they're just the opposite of truth. They are fear-fueled stories that you tell yourself. The next time you start to doubt yourself, take a moment to challenge that thought. Quantify the unrealized loss of potential and weigh it against the potential loss that may not occur.

Ask yourself, "What if just the opposite were true?"

What if what you have to say is important?

What if you were more than talented enough to pursue your goals?

What if you are more than prepared for that next role?

What if you have everything it takes to build that business?

What if your "what if" is an invitation to step into your purpose?

I've shared before that there is a difference between purpose and why. Purpose is our reason for being. Our why is our reason for doing. You can be clear about your purpose at any moment but still lose your motivation, your why, to do it. Doubt and fear are often the two biggest thieves of our motivation, and thusly, our purpose.

But remember, behind every why is a who—someone whom we envision when we need to remind ourselves why our why matters. It could be a family member, a friend, a mentor, someone from our past; it can even be ourselves. The question you must ask to find the strength and courage to overcome fear and doubt is, "Who is your who?"

One of my favorite characters in television is Max from *New Amsterdam*. He plays the chief medical director of the hospital the show is named after. On his first day in his role, he calls an assembly of the full hospital staff and introduces himself. He then abruptly asks all the cardiologists in the room to raise their hands. As their hands go up, he firmly says, "You're all fired!" A look of bewilderment and confusion pours over their faces as many of them take out their cell phones, likely to call their attorneys. Max continues, "Any person who puts profitability above patient care cannot work in my hospital." He points to the door and shouts, "Get out!"

He then asks the oncologists to raise their hands, and they slowly and cautiously do so. He responds, "How you have tried to battle one of the most challenging medical issues in human history with the limited resources this hospital has given you, is beyond me... Let's be doctors again," and he calls them back to their purpose.

In every episode of this show, Max is faced with a challenging situation that requires him to make unpopular decisions and overcome fear and doubt to achieve the purpose he can clearly see. At times he is faced with unimaginable circumstances personally, from the death of his wife to his own cancer prognosis. At times, he seems to lose his motivation, but remains steadfast and continues to step into his purpose each day. Why, you might ask?

We learn his sister was a patient in that hospital long before he was the medical director. She had a rare heart condition, and the hospital could have tried to serve her, but the equipment to do so was too expensive, and so she perished. Max's sister was the who behind his why.

Max was always clear about his purpose, his reason for being. But the challenges he had to overcome in the face of fear and doubt tried to rob him of moments to be who he knew he needed to be. His sister was his why, his reason for doing. She was the motivation inside him to overcome and keep moving forward.

Take a moment to think about moments of fear in your life that you have overcome. What was your motivation? Who were you thinking about when you stepped into that fear? Who was your who?

Perhaps you can't recall such a moment but you are faced with something now you know you either need to do or want to do and fear and doubt seem like insurmountable walls standing in your way. What might the impact be if you broke through those walls? Whose lives might be positively impacted because you overcame your fear and doubt? What difference might you make? Then ask yourself...

Is the pain of not making the difference you were created for greater than the pain of your fear?

I once heard a story of a speaker giving a presentation to a small group of people, and during the presentation, a dog in the room kept barking. The speaker paused and asked the dog owner if his dog was okay. The owner said, "Don't worry about it; keep going." The speaker continued and again the dog barked. The speaker asked the owner again about the dog, and the owner once again replied, "Don't worry about it; keep going." The speaker continued, and once again the dog barked.

The speaker, irritated, shouted, "What is up with your dog?"

The owner said, "He's sitting on a tack."

The speaker asked, "Why doesn't he get up?"

The owner replied, "I guess it doesn't hurt enough yet."

You may laugh at that joke, but are we not much like that dog? We see things in our lives and our world we want to change, but we don't take action. Until the pain of the status quo outweighs the pain of our fear, we won't move.

 Is the pain of not making the difference you were created for greater than the pain of your fear?

All that is meant for us in life awaits us on the other side of our fear. If you want to step into the fullness of who you were created to be, to fulfill every purpose you were created for, you will have to face the thief of fear at some point.

Your why has to be bigger than your won't.

Your "what if I fly" has to be bigger than your "what if I fall."

Like my friends Kent and Erica, you may have to just "do it afraid." Or as Dr. Maggie suggests, you may have to start "doubting your doubts."

Whichever one of these may resonate with you, one thing is certain: you will need to take action, and that action has to begin with a decision. A decision that means you are willing to be uncomfortable, to challenge the status quo, to step into the direction of your convictions, rather than remaining in the comfort of your complacency.

Four Thoughts to Overcome the Thief of Fear and Doubt

1. Identify your motive. Who is your who? Behind every why is a who, our true motivation. Whose voice—if they were to tell you to get up, to take that step, to move forward—would you listen to? Whose voice inspires you to step into action?

2. Ask yourself, "What if?" and envision the positive outcome for yourself and the lives of those you might impact. Ask yourself, "What if?" a second time and think of the potential lost impact if you choose to let fear prevent you from stepping into your calling or convictions.

3. Listen to the advice of my friend Kent and "do it afraid." Test your "knower." What do you feel within the fiber of your being? Often, our gut feelings, our instincts, are nudges that tell us what we know to be true, giving us confidence and direction.

4. As Maggie suggested, start "doubting your doubts." Remind yourself that your doubts are likely not inherently true. When you doubt yourself, test that doubt by asking yourself if the opposite is true and repeat the "What if?" exercise.

Thief #7
LIES

"A lie gets halfway around the world before the truth has a chance to get its pants on."

—Winston Churchill

We live in a world where lies seem to always speak louder than the truth, and therefore, we need to be vigilant in taking every thought captive and test the validity of not just what we are being told, but even more importantly, what we are telling ourselves.

In spring 2016, I took the biggest leap of faith in my professional career, a leap I did not feel equipped or even worthy to take. The time since has taught me so much about others, and even more so about myself. It has been rewarding and challenging. There have been hills and valleys. There have been moments I have fallen, and others where I experienced what it feels like to fly. When you have purpose and passion the hills and valleys don't matter; your purpose is level ground, and the rest is perception. We often care too much about the judgments of others, and their limiting beliefs make us question our self-worth and abilities. The lies we tell ourselves derail us from achieving that which we are passionate about, that which we are called to do, and the life we were created to live. They leave us standing on the cliff of life, looking out at the wide-open sky, asking ourselves, "What if?"

Much like we discussed in the previous chapter on fear, 91 percent of the things we fear might happen ultimately don't occur, and a large percentage of the negative thoughts we have about ourselves are simply not true. I don't have a specific percentage from an academic study to quantify that amount, but the truth is we are the largest inhibitors of our own potential simply because we choose to believe the lies we tell ourselves about ourselves.

For those of you who are married, you might have experienced telling your spouse how pretty they are, and the frustration of them not believing you and dismissing your compliment. No matter how genuine and true your compliment may be, the fact is the lies they are telling themselves is louder than the truth. She will not like that I am putting this in here, but I am going to anyway. I am constantly commenting on how unique and striking Amy's eyes are, not boastfully to others, but just to her. Even after seventeen years of marriage, I still find myself staring at them. Partly because I can't help myself, but partly because I always want her to know that I see her. I want to help her combat the lies in her head.

Here is the part she would not want me to share, but I will anyway. I have lost count of how many times we have been in public, and a random stranger has stopped us and said directly to her that her eyes are stunning. I'm not making that up. It happens often; it just happened again last week when we were greeted by a hostess at a restaurant. But no matter how often strangers tell her that, the lies in her head speak louder, and she is not alone. The amount of people who struggle with their self-image, self-confidence, and self-worth is staggering, and it's not just women.

In fall 2023, I had the opportunity to emcee the Culture Forum at San Diego State University, and event that brought a hundred C-Suite leaders from around the world together to focus on building great cultures. One of the speakers, Scott Blanchard, the son of one of my career-long mentors Ken Blanchard, talked about openly addressing the things that most people are struggling with in their minds that they feel they can't talk about in the workplace, particularly the lies they tell themselves about what they can and cannot express openly.

Scott conducted a poll in the room, asking people to select one thing they struggle most with not talking about. The topics included many "taboo" subjects, including religion, politics, sexual orientation, and mental health. When the poll was finished, more people had answered "mental health" compared to all the other topics combined. In fact, two out of three people in the room struggled with mental health, and he knew from doing this before that this would be the result of his poll. He even put us in groups of three prior to taking the poll, and after the results were revealed, he said, "Look to your left and to your right. Two of the three of you are struggling." This was a room filled with many accomplished high-ranking executives! At dinner the night before, Scott shared with me that his struggle was his inspiration for choosing this topic, and during his talk revealed that to the room in a beautiful demonstration of vulnerability and honesty. In choosing to confront the thief of lies, Scott stepped into an insightful moment of purpose that impacted a hundred people from around the world and has stuck with me since.

Amongst the mental health crisis, one of the most rapidly growing topics I find people struggling with is imposter syndrome. My dear friend Gary Frey wrote a fantastic book entitled *Silence the Imposter*, where he helps readers identify when the imposter is attacking and offers seven tactics for how to silence it. If you find yourself struggling with imposter syndrome, I highly recommend his book as a follow-up to this read. Like Scott, Gary chose to step into his struggle, to confront the lies in his mind, and in doing so, stepped into his purpose and has impacted countless lives through his work since.

Our self-talk has the power to either thrust us into our purpose and potential or prevent us from stepping into it. I have personally found that some of the most impactful authors and speakers are those who write and speak from the pain and experience of their struggles. If you find yourself struggling with something you are hiding, that struggle might be an invitation to step into a moment of purpose, to say something, write something, or do something that will help others who might be struggling with the same thing, and in doing so, you will experience a freedom that can only be found by fighting the lies with the truth.

I recently researched common lies that we tell both ourselves and others, and decided to get real with myself to see how often I say these common phrases. Read these and see if any of them resonate with you.

"I'm fine."
"I know what I'm doing."
"I don't need help."
"Everything is great."
"I have to be perfect."
"I don't have a choice."
"I don't have enough time."
"I am too young."
"I'm too old."
"I'm not good enough."
"I don't matter."

If I am being honest, I have said every one of these phrases at some point in my life. Have you?

It's astonishing how much we lie to ourselves and to others. A 2023 study by Bright Futures shared these staggering statistics.

60 percent of people admit to telling people they are "fine" when they are actually struggling.

An average person lies one or two times a day.

60 percent of people lie at least once in a ten-minute conversation.

Men lie six times a day on average, while women lie three times a day on average.

40 percent of people lie on their resumes.

90 percent of people lie on their online dating profiles.

80 percent of women admit to lying to their partner about their spending habits.

50 percent of teenagers admit to lying to their parents about their whereabouts.

81 percent of people lie about their height, weight, or age online.

People are more likely to lie over the phone than face-to-face.

64 percent of people lie about their personal accomplishments.

63 percent of people lie about their emotions to save face.

27 percent of people lie out of fear of consequences.

23 percent of people lie to protect themselves or others from harm.

20 percent of people lie to avoid embarrassment or shame.

My dear friend and colleague Ron Carucci wrote what I believe to be one of the most comprehensive, challenging, and honest books ever written. It's entitled *To Be Honest: Lead with the Power of Truth, Justice, and Purpose*. It's a masterpiece of a literary work that will challenge you to get real with who you actually are, compared to who you proclaim yourself to be.

Ron suggests we are living in a trust recession, and the statistics I just shared would suggest he is right. We have perhaps quickly become the most dishonest society in the history of the world, and it has created more damage and robbed more people of their purpose and potential than we can possibly calculate.

Lying severely damages trust and relationships and can have significant negative effects on mental health. Research has found that individuals who frequently lie experience more anxiety, depression, and stress than those who are more honest.

I shared in the introduction of this book that one of my favorite verses has always been, "The truth shall set you free." Every time I have been tempted to lie for even the smallest reason, I call that verse to mind, and every time the consequences I feared, the outcomes I envisioned never materialized. Each time I felt free of the lies I had been telling myself.

Many people lie to protect their ego and their reputation, most commonly in the realm of business. But amongst the crowd, there are some sage examples of honesty in the business world we can learn from. Garry Ridge, whom I know I have quoted often, boldly shares publicly that the three most powerful words he has ever learned are "I don't know." Make no mistake, Garry is confident about who he is, as the former CEO of WD40 Company for twenty-five years, and now chairman emeritus, he used to introduce himself as the "consciously incompetent, probably wrong, and roughly right CEO of WD-40 Company." He knew that he did not know everything, and that often, he didn't always get it right. In admitting at times that he did not know the answer to a question, rather than letting his ego get in the way, he created an opportunity to learn something new and fostered an environment where it was okay for people to be their most honest selves. The result was a highly engaged, highly creative, high-performing culture at WD40 Company.

By being honest with himself and with others, he inspired others to be honest with themselves and with each other. One of my favorite things that Garry has taught me and countless others is to redefine failure as "learning moments." I almost included an entire chapter on failure as being a thief of purpose but ended up not doing so because I no longer look at failure as a thief, for when we choose to look at our failures as learning moments, we can find purpose for them and in them.

WD-40 Company was built on learning moments through failure.

In 1953, in a small lab in San Diego, California, the fledgling Rocket Chemical Company and its staff of three set out to create a line of rust-prevention solvents and degreasers for use in the aerospace industry. The first formula failed. The second formula failed. The tenth, twentieth, and thirtieth formula failed. But the fortieth formula worked, and "Water Displacement, fortieth formula," better known as WD40, was born.

If you visit their headquarters, they have a staircase at the entrance that has Rocket Chemical Company written on the first step, the numbers one through thirty-nine staggered up the staircase, and "success" written on the top step. A daily reminder to all who walk them that failures are just learning moments.

We can learn a lot from Garry's leadership and the example of a company whose product is sitting on a shelf of almost every home and building across the world. It is inevitable that you will mess up. You are not going to get it right all the time. Even after reading this book, you will still struggle with many if not all of these thieves. But when that happens, it's essential that you recognize that as a learning moment and ask yourself what you could have done differently and what you will do next time.

The more honest we can be with ourselves and with others, the more opportunities we will create to step into moments of purpose. The more we allow our fear and ego to get in the way, the more opportunities we will miss. We live in a world that has conditioned us to think that vulnerability is for the weak. The truth is, only the strong find the strength to be vulnerable.

 "When we choose to look at our failures as learning moments, we can find purpose for them and in them."

One of the exercises that Ron Carucci takes you through in his work is having you take a deep look at your past to understand your wiring and upbringing. In 2024, he spoke at The Purpose Summit on the topic of "Facing Our Origin Stories." It was a transformative talk that has since been made public and you can watch it online. As he shared, I realized how many lies I had told myself over the years, and the excuses I had made that had robbed me of so much that I could have achieved and experienced if I only had these insights sooner. If you are reading these words right now, you can benefit from such insights and change your future.

C.S. Lewis once said, "You can't go back and change the beginning, but you can start where you are and change the ending."

Whatever lies that you have told yourself in the past, I implore you to recognize them for what they are: lies. Starting where you are right now, I encourage you to get honest with who you really are and what you are capable of. Pick up Ron Carucci's book *To Be Honest* and discover the truths about yourself that will set you free and unleash your potential and purpose.

Four Thoughts to Overcome the Thief of Lies

1. Recognize that most, if not all, of the negative thoughts you have about yourself or the fearful situations you believe are simply not true and will most likely not manifest. If you find yourself in a spiral of negative self-talk, share your struggle with someone you trust. They will help you recognize the lie for what it is and speak life into you, and when they do, believe them.

2. Track your self-talk. How often are you lying to yourself and to others? Ask yourself the common phrases we discussed in this chapter. Just reading through them a couple of times alone will help trigger your attention the next time you say them and will challenge you to test their validity and be more truthful.

3. Turn your failures into learning moments. If you make a mistake, ask yourself what you learned and what you can apply next time. Each time you find yourself struggling with one of the thieves in this book is a learning moment. Identifying which thief you are struggling with, even if you failed to confront it in that moment, you will build a deeper conviction to confront it the next time it shows itself.

4. Revisit your past, but don't live there. There is much we can learn from our upbringing, about how we are wired and conditioned, and the experiences that have shaped us, and all too often we allow those events to be the justification for why we are the way we are. Remember C.S. Lewis' words, "You can't go back and change the beginning, but you can start where you are and change the ending."

Thief #8
GUILT

"Have you forgiven yourself yet?"

—Dr. Mark Goulston

Over the years, I have had the opportunity to be a guest on a few podcasts, and many of those conversations have left an indelible mark on my life. In 2022, I had the honor and pleasure of spending time with one of the most wonderful human beings I have ever met, Dr. Mark Goulston, a renowned psychiatrist, author, and executive coach. During most podcasts, the host usually wants to talk about my work and passion on the topic of purpose or about my books or the story of PurposePoint and The Purpose Summit. But this conversation was different. Mark quickly in his questioning pulled back layers of my life that I didn't even know were there, to help me realize a struggle deep within me that I didn't know existed. Guilt.

When I was five years old, my parents divorced and I went to live with my grandparents, whom I became attached to. It was a tough and dark time in my childhood, comforted only by the smell of my grandmother's gravy (known as pasta sauce to most), which filled her home most days, or the warmth of sitting next to her with a cup of coffee in hands, at what many would consider far too young of an age to be drinking coffee. I am convinced that my infatuation with coffee had more to do with the comfort of this memory than the actual coffee itself. Equally memorable and comforting was sitting next to my grandfather, curled up under his arm holding a

magnifying glass while he read books in large print night after night,
with the sounds of either Frank Sinatra or Dean Martin playing in the
background or the evening news on the television. Even writing these
words, remembering these moments, feels like a warm soft blanket
comforting me from the coldness of that time of my life.

During my conversation with Mark, we spent a lot of time talking
about my grandparents, how selfless they were, and the contrast
between the two different worlds I was experiencing in my
childhood. While I have known for some time that my passion
and desire to help and serve others stems from watching my
grandparents' example of how they lived, I soon realized in our
conversation the weight of guilt that I carried from choices that I
made in the fallout of my parents' divorce. I will spare you the details
of those choices, but it's clear to me now that the gravity of those
decisions devalued my sense of worth and purpose. I felt tarnished
and unusable, like damaged goods beyond repair.

For years, I blamed my parents and struggled to forgive them, and
I even felt guilty about that. But as time passed, and I started to
see a greater purpose for my life unfold because of all of the things
that happened in my childhood, I learned to forgive them and
move on, but I didn't realize that I had never forgiven myself. I had
been carrying a weight of guilt with me for thirty-seven years that
I needed to let go of if I was going to step into the fullness of my
purpose and potential. Mark helped me realize that.

Mark and I became friends following that conversation and got
to know each other better over the next two years through the
Marshall Goldsmith 100 Coaches community that we were both
honored members of. During those two years, Mark became ill,
and true to who Mark was, even in his most challenging season
of life, he continued to pour into others. He started a new podcast
entitled *I'm Dying to Tell You*. He knew his time was short and had

so much yet to give to the world. Just before the week of Christmas in 2023, Mark was admitted to the hospital for a bone marrow transplant, and he could not be more optimistic. He even recorded new episodes right from his hospital bed. His last one was entitled, "I need your help." He was struggling with finding the strength to get up out of bed each day, as he was directed to do as a part of his recovery, and in that episode said this:

"I need you to do me a favor, I need you to do something today that you don't want to do, that you know you need to do. And If I know you are doing that thing that you don't want to do that you need to do, then I will find the strength to get up out of bed every day."

He posted that episode on LinkedIn with a challenge to respond in the comments on what it is that each of us would do. I commented, "Mark, it's a deal. You once told me that I need to forgive myself for scars and pains that I have long carried with me. Today and every day after, I will do my best to lay those down."

He responded a few days later, "How's the forgiving yourself going, Davin?"

I had not yet responded before learning that shortly after he wrote those words, he contracted an infection and left us on the morning of New Year's Eve, 2023.

Doug Guthrie, a fellow MG100 coach and now dear friend, perhaps said it best in his tribute to Mark when he said, "His greatest talent was his ability to channel his incisive insights to take people deep into self-reflective conversations while cloaking those insights in humility that made those around him feel safe."

Letting go of the past is a common theme we talk about in the MG100, and as I mentioned in the last chapter, it's okay to revisit it, but don't live there. Revisiting our past can provide us with learning moments to step into our present purpose.

I recently had a conversation with another dear friend of mine, Charlie Malouf. I first met Charlie when I saw a LinkedIn post celebrating a "Purpose Day" that he and his leadership team had hosted for their "Memory Makers," which is the name they have chosen to give their employees at their company, Broad River Retail. Truly one of the most remarkable cultures I have ever seen, and some of the most amazing people I have ever met. You can read more about their culture in *Finding Purpose at Work* in the chapter entitled "What Good Looks Like."

Charlie and I talk a lot about memories, both the good ones and the ones we can learn from. He and Garry Ridge share some of the same incredible leadership traits, and both have become tremendous friends whom I have given carte blanche permission to challenge me when I need to be challenged.

In my recent conversation with Charlie, I shared how I was struggling with patience in being the father I should be to my son, particularly when it comes to sports. It didn't matter what sport I tried to teach Bennett; he did not handle failure well. A simple missed shot in soccer or hockey or dropped ball in football or baseball would send him off in a tantrum, and he would quit as quickly as we began. Every time he would quit, I would also want to quit. I had little tolerance for his tantrums, and Amy constantly challenged me to be more patient and bolder with him.

Because of my upbringing and the time I spent as a child at my grandparents', I didn't have many memories of playing sports with my parents, so I would often make the excuse that I didn't know how to teach Bennett because I was never taught; I had to teach myself. But that was a skin of a reason, stuffed with a lie. The truth was, I didn't want to because I couldn't handle his impatience. Talk about the pot calling the kettle black.

I shared this story vulnerably with my friend Charlie and admitted that I was ashamed and stuck in my guilt of not being the father that I had always envisioned I could be. In fact, when Amy and I first got married, I told her that I wanted to have kids by the age of thirty because when my son grows up I wanted to have to opportunity to play sports with him, and I didn't want to be fifty when I did. Little did I know that what my mind thought my body could do and what it actually could do started to disconnect after age forty!

Charlie, who had recently lost his own father, challenged me. He shared his childhood, guilt, and regrets, and a beautiful redemptive story of the final moments he was blessed to spend with his dad by his bedside. He encouraged me at that moment to let go of my guilt and asked me what I was doing when I got home that evening. Before I could answer, he said, "Go outside and play soccer with your boy. Step into that purpose you are always talking about, be patient with him, and make some memories together. You will never get this time back."

I went home that night and did exactly as Charlie encouraged me to do, and since that time, soccer has become Bennett's favorite sport. In fact, he practically lives in a Messi jersey, which just this morning we told him he needs to wash because it's all he wears, and he has become quite good. This past season, he was the top scorer on his team, with several multiple-goal games. I don't know if he will become the next Messi, but I do know that like all of us, he has the capability to be if he doesn't let the thieves of this life rob him of his potential.

While I take great joy in his love for the sports I take no credit for his accomplishments, and he still has a tantrum every now and then.

But when he does, I remember my conversation with my friend Charlie, who helped me confront my guilt and my failures, and step into my purpose as a father. I still don't get it right all the time, but each failure has become a learning moment that has given me more patience than I previously had to be the father I have always wanted to be and envisioned I could be.

The voices of those in our lives have great power to convict us or condemn us. Condemnation never leads to purpose, and conviction almost always does. Charlie's words convicted me greatly.

 "Condemnation never leads to purpose, and conviction almost always does."

If you are experiencing guilt, that is the voice of condemnation and a thief of purpose. The key is to turn that condemnation into conviction. I'll quote C.S. Lewis again: *"You can't go back and change the beginning, but you can start where you are and change the ending."*

One of my favorite books of all time is *The Freedom of Self-Forgetfulness* by the late Timothy Keller; it's also the shortest book I have ever read. It was first shared with me by my friend Dwight Eberts, who would buy dozens of copies and give them to everyone he knew, and now I know why. When we launched PurposePoint, I gave every person on my team a copy. Dwight and I have discussed Keller's book at length, partly because it is so impactful but mainly because we both find it so relatable. We have both struggled with the acceptance of grace, bound by the guilt of our past mistakes, allowing them to define us, each individually in our own way.

I know I have recommended a lot of books to you, and for good reason. It's been said you will be the same person you are five years from now except for two things: the books you read and the people you surround yourself with. I have found that to personally be a profound truth and realization in my life.

While we may change as a person, which I certainly have over the years, thanks to the books I have read and the people who have come into my life, Keller offers in his work that our identity does not change. We are not defined by our failures or our successes. Your value does not go up or down like the stock market based upon your actions. Your value, identity, and purpose are fixed within the very blueprint by which you were created.

Keller, an accomplished Christian author and pastor, is someone I identify with, and wherever you may be in your faith, I would offer there is great value in his argument, perspective, and work as a whole. Even though he was a bestselling author of multiple books, he did not allow that status to define him. He remained humble, recognizing his identity was not tied to the height of his success, nor to the weight of his failures. In his humility he didn't diminish his successes either, quoting C.S. Lewis as well, who also said, "True humility is not thinking less of oneself, but rather thinking of oneself less."

Read that quote again. How many times have you been offered a compliment for something you have achieved, and immediately dismissed it to be humble? I have many times.

I often wonder if the reason I have struggled with letting go of the past, my failures, and my shortcomings is subconsciously intentional. What if the reason I have held onto such guilt for so long was to keep me humble, not as Lewis defines true humility, but by how society conditions us to be humble, by thinking less of ourselves, rather than thinking of ourselves less?

Since reading Keller's book multiple times, I have discovered great freedom, hence the title of his work. I have learned not to let my past guilt bind me or define me. I have learned to accept grace, which has completely washed my guilt away. I have learned that it is okay to celebrate my accomplishments, while also not allowing those to define me either. I have learned to think of myself less, which has allowed me to focus more on others, and ultimately to recognize and step into more moments of purpose.

I mentioned earlier that purpose is plural and momentary, and it can often feel like we have multiple purposes competing for our attention. While raising our kids when they were younger, Amy would often experience "mom guilt"—that sense that I am not doing enough for or spending enough time with my kids because of all the other stuff I have to get done. There is no question that the hardest and most underpaid job on the planet is being a mom, and moms, I honestly don't know how you do it, and I applaud you!

The number of priorities that I have watched Amy juggle is incomprehensible to me. From taking care of our home, cleaning, doing laundry, grocery shopping, planning and cooking meals, buying clothes for our kids, coordinating birthday parties, buying gifts, the list goes on and on, all while trying to find time for herself, not to mention accomplishing her own goals and dreams beyond being the great mother she is, and somehow, she feels guilt?

Think about the amount of purpose moments were fulfilled just in that list! (Gentlemen, if you are blessed to have a similar amazing woman in your life and you have not thanked her recently, or made her feel seen and appreciated, put this book down right now, and go cherish her! In doing so, you will also be fulfilling your purpose!)

I have assured Amy many times that her intentions have always been pure, and not once were our kids ever slighted or cheated on time and attention because the truth is she was pouring all of herself into them in multiple ways, even if they didn't realize or appreciate it.

One of the silent tactics guilt uses is for us to judge ourselves by the way others might see us, in this case by how our kids might see her. Even though they had never expressed such thoughts, Amy felt them all the same.

We tend to judge others by their actions and not their intentions. Because we do so, we also feel judged by our actions and not our intentions. But what if we laid that judgment down, on both sides, and looked at intentions?

When we choose to look at our intentions rather than our actions, guilt flees. Likewise, when we choose to understand the intentions of others rather than just looking at their actions, judgment flees.

There is a reason our judgment system was based on the premise of innocent until proven guilty. But the thief would have you believe you are guilty, no matter the amount of evidence around you that would prove otherwise.

Make no mistake, there is a battle raging for your self-worth. Your ability to step into the fullness of your purpose and potential, to fulfill all that is meant for you in this life, hangs in the balance of that verdict. The great news is the verdict is already in, and if you choose to read Keller's book, and understand the premise behind it, you will experience the freedom of self-forgetfulness.

Whatever guilt you have been holding onto, it's time to let it go. Whatever failures you have been dwelling upon, it's time to relabel them as learning moments. I want to encourage and empower you today to put the weight of your guilt and your failures under your feet and to use them as stepping stones to rise.

Your past failures will fuel your present intentions, and you will find that they will give your future accompaniments purpose and meaning. The most important step in becoming who we need to be is letting go of who we used to be.

Four Thoughts to Overcome the Thief of Guilt

1. What do you need to forgive yourself for? What have you been holding onto for so long that has felt like an anchor keeping you grounded in your past? Remember the words of my late friend Dr. Mark Goulston and ask yourself, "Have you forgiven yourself yet?"

2. What failures have you made excuses for that you need to confront? Remember, an excuse is the skin of a reason stuffed with a lie. What lie are you telling yourself that is preventing you from overcoming that failure? Relabel that failure as a learning moment. Recognize that you have an opportunity to try again and that you cannot get time back. Take advantage of the time you have while you have it.

3. Where do you place your identity? If it is in your failures or your successes, recognize that neither defines you. I encourage you to pick up a copy of Tim Keller's book *The Freedom of Self-Forgetfulness* so that you too can learn not to let your past guilt bind or define you, learn to celebrate your accomplishments, while also not allowing those to define you either, and learn to think of yourself less so you can focus more on others and ultimately recognize and step into more moments of purpose.

4. Focus on intentions. Don't allow your actions, or the perceived thoughts of your actions by others, to overshadow your intentions. Extend that same grace to others. Remember that when we choose to look at our intentions rather than our actions, guilt flees. Likewise, when we choose to understand the intentions of others rather than just looking at their actions, judgment flees.

Thief #9

QUITTING

"It's always too early to quit."

—Norman Vincent Peale

Amy and I were on the couch one evening during the first week of January, discussing our goals for the new year and our plans to achieve them. There is something about the start of the new year that enables us all to let our past failures go and motivates us to start fresh with a clean slate. I had not accomplished my reading, writing, or workout goals for 2023, and was determined to do so in 2024. So, I laid out my plan about how I would get up early each morning, spend the first hour of my day reading, the second hour writing, and the third hour working out, all between six a.m. and nine a.m. Amy lovingly reminded me that I had a similar routine to start 2023, and asked, "How did that work out for you last year?" It occurred to me at that moment that it wasn't my routine that was the problem—it was the frequency and, ultimately, my commitment to it.

There is a difference between determination and commitment. I may have been determined in my heart and mind to accomplish those goals, but I didn't follow through with action and eventually gave up on those goals. It's a far too common story; gyms are packed with millions of people in January who quit showing up in February. It's amazing how much unrealized potential is lost so quickly. It's easy to say what we want to do, what we want to accomplish, who we want to become, but often we fail to remind ourselves of our why behind our goals to keep us motivated. This is why we need accountability, people outside of ourselves who we are committed to and can share our goals with who will hold us accountable and will remind us of our why when we want to give up.

I also shared my plan with my colleague Lisa, who has a gift of making sure in our office that the ball doesn't get dropped and we always follow through and do what we say we will do for those we serve. She made it simple for me. She said, "Starting today, you are not allowed in the office until you have accomplished your reading, writing, and workout goals." Sure enough, the next day, I woke up, read for an hour, wrote for an hour, and worked out for an hour, and sent her a message that read, "Day one complete!" She said, "You may now enter the office."

Far too often we quit our goals when we break a streak or we are not perfect in our pursuit of them. My devotional app has a little ticker at the top that keeps track of how many consecutive days I am in it. Each year I aim to get that number to 365, and each year I fail. My highest streak was once 172 days, and then I missed a day, and the ticker went back to zero. My streak was over, I wasn't perfect, and I was ready to throw in the towel on my devotional goal. But instead, I started again and set a new goal to see if I could beat 172.

Perhaps many of us are more of a perfectionist than we would like to admit. But as I shared earlier, perfectionism can also be a thief of purpose. I love how Jon Acuff put it when he said, "This is the first lie that perfectionism tells you about your goals: Quit if it isn't perfect."

I recommend we stop making New Year's resolutions and we start making new day resolutions. If you failed yesterday, start again and every day after. Purpose knows no failure or defeat; it is the voice in those moments that inspires us to keep moving forward. What happened yesterday doesn't matter. Each day is a new opportunity to be who we were created to be. Win the day.

 | *"Purpose knows no failure or defeat; it is the voice in those moments that inspires us to keep moving forward."*

I firmly believe that each of us is meant to accomplish our goals not just for ourselves, but for the impact our lives are supposed to have on others, and perhaps even on the world. I often look back at decisions I made not to quit, even in times when I was embattled by setback after setback, and disappointment after disappointment, most of which was beyond my control. In fact, the only thing that I could control in many of these moments was my commitment to keep trying, to keep moving forward. I shudder to think how much impact might have been lost on the lives of others if I had quit, simply because things just got too hard, and I was emotionally exhausted by defeat and disappointment.

One of my favorite examples of this is captured in the life of Abraham Lincoln.

When he was seven years old, his family was forced out of their home and off their farm. Like other boys his age, he was expected to work to help support the family.

When he was nine, his mother died.

At the age of twenty-two, the company he worked for went bankrupt and he lost his job.

At twenty-three, he ran for state legislature in a field of thirteen candidates. He came in eighth.

At twenty-four, he borrowed money to start a business with a friend. By the end of the year, the business failed. The local sheriff seized his possessions to pay off his debt. His partner soon died, penniless, and he assumed his partner's share of debt as well. He spent the next several years of his life paying it off.

At twenty-five, he ran for state legislature again. This time he won.

At twenty-six, he was engaged to be married. But his fiancé died before the wedding. The next year he plunged into a depression and suffered a nervous breakdown.

At twenty-nine, he sought to become the speaker of the state legislature. He was defeated.

At thirty-four, he campaigned for a US congressional seat, representing his district. He lost.

At thirty-five, he ran for Congress again. This time he won. He went to Washington and did a good job.

At thirty-nine, when his term ended, he was out of a job again. There was a one-term-limit rule in his party.

At forty, he tried to get a job as commissioner of the General Land Office. He was rejected.

At forty-five, he campaigned for the US Senate, representing his state. He lost by six electoral votes.

At forty-seven, he was one of the contenders for the vice-presidential nomination at his party's national convention. He lost.

At forty-nine, he ran for the same US Senate seat a second time. And for the second time, he lost.

Two years later, at the age of fifty-one, after a lifetime of failure, disappointment, and loss, Abraham Lincoln was elected the sixteenth president of the United States.

The next time you consider giving up when faced with a setback, consider this story. Imagine how the world would be different today if Lincoln gave up after his first setback...or his second...or his tenth.

Multiple studies have shown that only 8–9 percent of people accomplish their goals in any given year. Most people simply quit; they give up on what they want to achieve or who they want to become, and perhaps even worse, who they were meant to become.

Every person who has achieved something of notoriety or made a significant difference in this world, like President Lincoln, has had to make the choice not to quit. The more noble the pursuit, the greater the temptation will be to give up when the going gets tough. We can easily grow weary in well-doing, but our vision to make a difference must be greater than our temptation to quit.

I want to challenge you in reading this to ask yourself this question: "Who am I meant to become?"

Pause and read that again and be sure to use the right word. Notice I didn't ask who you wanted to become. Ask yourself again, "Who am I *meant* to become?"

Every person we have ever read about who has made a difference in this world, like the rest of humanity, was a child at one point in their lives, who grew into the person they became, not by circumstance, but by choice. Our circumstances don't define us; our choices do.

 "Your vision to make a difference must be greater than your temptation to quit."

That said, I believe there is a plan for each of our lives. In fact, I would say there are multiple plans for our lives, and our choices determine the plan that becomes our story.

When I was in elementary school I hated to read, kind of ironic since I became an author and avid reader. Each month the Scholastic bus would show up at our school and we were required to pick out a book to read for the month. At the front of the bus was a small spinning rack with a selection of "Choose Your Own Adventure" books. I always grabbed one of these books because they were short to begin with, and depending on the choices I made in the story, the book could be finished quickly. I always marveled at how those little books were written. You as the reader are the main character in the book, and each page sets you in a narrative with a choice at the end of that page. The choice you make determines which page in the book you turn to next and how the story continues to play out.

This is a great illustration of our lives. Our story is already written and there are multiple ways it can play out. Each day is like a page in one of those books. Each day we are presented with countless choices in any given moment: how we spend our time, what we choose to eat, what we choose to read, who we choose to listen to, what we choose to say, where we choose to go, where we choose to work, what we choose to buy, the list is endless. But the most important choice we can make each day is whether we choose to quit, and as Napoleon Hill once said, "It's always too early to quit."

We are a product of our choices, and while life can deal us unforeseen and unimaginable circumstances, even then we have a choice in how we face them, and who we choose to be in the midst of them. Some of the most inspiring stories we have ever read and movies that we have seen are of people who had to face and overcome tremendous adversity, and in the process of overcoming, they became who they were meant to be.

One day you will tell a story of how you overcame what you are going through, and it will be the inspiration someone else needs to overcome whatever they are going through.

In every challenge I have faced in my life, in every circumstance, I have learned to stop asking *why* and to start asking *what*.

Instead of asking yourself why this is happening, start asking, "What is this happening for?" Perhaps even more importantly, start asking who. *"Who is this happening for?"*

I love the words of my friend Jacob Brown, author of *Fail Forward Mentality*, who once said during his talk at The Purpose Summit, "We must use every failure, every adversity, every hardship we go through in life as lessons to grow thicker skin, and ultimately to help others."

A life of purpose is about pursuing significance, not just success. We become who we are meant to be not when we pursue our own ambitions—far too many people give up on their ambitions—but rather when we relentlessly pursue meeting the most urgent need we see in the world. It is our burning desire to meet that need that will give us the strength to keep moving forward when we want to give up the most.

Those words might sound like motivational rhetoric, but they could not be truer, and the book you now hold in your hands is proof of that. Even as I write these words, I am overcoming the most challenging year of my professional life and have lost count of how many times I have wanted to quit. I often daydream about dropping it all, closing up shop, disappearing from social media, moving our family to Italy, buying a vineyard, and making wine for the rest of my life. Sounds audacious and completely selfish? It absolutely is. As peaceful as that may sound, what an empty and bitter life that would be, devoid of meaning and purpose, and completely unfair to my family. Sure, I could become a successful winemaker, but where is the significance of that? No, the significance is found in the words you are reading now, in my choice not to give up, to keep pressing forward, to overcome the immense adversity that I am currently facing in my life, so that you might read these words and overcome the adversity in your life, to become who you were created to be.

Perseverance is the foundational ingredient of significance. One of my favorite verses in life that has continued to propel me forward reads: "Perseverance must finish its work so that you may be mature and complete, not lacking anything."

I want you to focus on those last three words: *not lacking anything.* Forget about material possessions because in the end they will not be a part of your story; only what you have done for others, how you made them feel, and who you helped them become, will remain when you are gone. What might your story be lacking if you choose to quit, if you choose not to let perseverance finish its work?

I almost quit in the year 2024. It had been a hard year on multiple fronts. My bride was overcoming health challenges and we were up to our necks in medical bills. Our daughter was facing a tough time at school, which eventually led us to decide that this would be her last year in that school. PurposePoint was facing its hardest financial year ever, and I had personally poured all that we had, except for the equity from our home, into it. I decided to dissolve the company structure and partnership we had put in place, and to assume the debt, risk, and liability of the company to set my partners free and avoid bankruptcy. We were struggling financially, both personally and professionally, and had already committed to contracts for Purpose Summit 2024 that we were not on pace to meet our financial commitments. The weight that I was carrying was indescribably heavy. It all felt like a terrible bad dream that I was pleading to wake up from, and there was no rest in sight.

Normally I take a break to reset after The Purpose Summit, but this year when we returned from PS24 in Charlotte, I had no shortage of big rocks on my plate. There was no time for rest. We were in the process of moving to Charlotte. I had to find a home for our family, get our home ready to list in just a couple of weeks, all while preparing to speak at two conferences in that same time period: GWIS in London on the topic of Workforce Transformation and Small Giants in Detroit on the topic of Enduring—how appropriate. Oh, I almost forgot, I also had to get this manuscript finished and off to the publisher in the next seven weeks. To say I was running on fumes is a gross understatement. I was time-poor, cash-poor, over-committed, and over-leveraged. But I just kept hanging on *"What if?"*

The day before my talk at Small Giants in Detroit, my dear friend Dwight Eberts walked into my office and handed me a sign that he had carried with him for some time. It was a large black canvas with a single word bolded in white that read, "Perseverance." Under that word it read in smaller letters, "Steadfastness in doing something despite difficulty or delay in achieving success." He had a front-row seat to my journey over the past seven years, and he knew every intimate detail of every struggle that I had battled through and was still battling through. In fact, I had told only two people in my life, my bride, Amy, and Dwight, just days before the summit that I was done, that I couldn't do this anymore. I just wanted the struggle to be over, the pressure to be lifted. I wanted to quit.

But then came the survey feedback results from Purpose Summit 2024, and the testimonies of impact had resoundingly answered my "what if" question. While financially the summit did not achieve its goals, to say that the summit was a transformative success for the lives and organizations of those who experienced it would be an understatement. My convictions were renewed, my doubts removed, and my confidence restored, knowing that the thieves I had been battling all along had failed to rob me of the purpose and impact that I had to fight for. The battle was far from over. I still had to figure out how to make the summit financially viable and sustainable, but there was one thing that I knew for certain: quitting was no longer an option, and I felt the support of a growing community around me, each whose face and voice became my why to press forward.

As Norman Vincent Peale said, "It's always too early to quit." Many people quit a goal or dream just when they are on the brink of a breakthrough or it becoming a reality. It's usually when the challenges become the hardest that we're often closer to our achieving our goals than we believe ourselves to be.

In 1952, a woman named Florence Chadwick decided to attempt the twenty-six-mile swim between the California coastline and Catalina Island. During her swim, Chadwick swam with a team whose job was to keep an eye out for sharks and to be prepared to help support her in the event of unexpected cramps, injury, or fatigue. About fifteen hours into her swim, a thick fog began to set in, clouding Chadwick's vision. Her confidence began to fade. Her mother happened to be in one of the boats at the time as Chadwick signaled to her team she didn't think she could complete the swim.

She swam for another hour before deciding to call it quits. As she sat in the teetering boat she discovered if she'd just continued on for another mile, she would have reached Catalina Island.

Two months after Chadwick's failed attempt she tried the swim once more. Once again, a thick fog set in. Learning from her previous attempt, this time she had a mental image of the shoreline in her mind and used that image to keep pressing forward. Chadwick reached the shoreline and even made the swim two more times! Chadwick would go on to become the first woman to swim the English Channel in both directions, both in record times.

Maybe you don't have a failed attempt like Chadwick to learn from, or an image of how close you were to achieving a goal to keep you moving forward when the fog sets in or the challenges become the hardest. This is where the powerful question of "What if?" can help you. When tempted to quit, envision the impact of what it is you are fighting for, the goal you are trying to reach, or the purpose you are striving to fulfill. Keep that image fixed solidly in your mind and use it to keep moving forward. Like Chadwick you just might be much closer than you believe yourself to be.

Four Thoughts to Overcome the Thief of Quitting

1. Who do you have in your life that you can share your goals, your
    dreams, or your vision of impact with, who will help you stay
    accountable and steadfast in achieving them? Identify those
    people in your life, and don't just share with them, but be clear
    as to why achieving those things is important and give them
    permission to never let you quit. If you break a streak, start over
    and treat every day like it's January 1.

2. Like President Lincoln, remember that failure, defeat, and
    setbacks are all a part of the journey that ultimately leads to
    accomplishment, and perhaps historic impact. Failure is never
    fatal or final unless you choose it to be. If Lincoln's story doesn't
    inspire you, find another. There is no shortage of historical
    overcoming that you can reference to keep you inspired to try
    and try again.

3. Remember that perseverance is the foundational ingredient
    of significance. *"Perseverance must finish its work so that you
    may be mature and complete, not lacking anything."* Read that
    again: *"not lacking anything."* It's all a part of the story. Often our
    purpose is our story. Like Lincoln or Chadwick, your story might
    serve a purpose to inspire others long after you are gone.

4. Keep asking, "What if?" Envision the impact of what it is you are
    fighting for, the goal you are trying to reach, or the purpose you
    are striving to fulfill. Keep that image fixed solidly in your mind
    and use it to keep moving forward.

Thief #10

SUCCESS

"Not all success is a gift, particularly if it costs you what is most important."

—Buck Jacobs

One day while driving my kids to school, they both asked me, "Dad, who is the most famous person you know?" That was a tough question to answer.

I replied, "That all depends on what you mean by famous."

They both responded the same, "You know, famous—rich and successful."

I replied, "Well, those are different things. You don't need to be rich to be famous or successful." A debate quickly ensued.

I asked them to name some people they considered famous. They named various social influencers with millions of followers and a celebrity pop artist who just finished making a billion dollars on a world stadium tour. I acknowledged that they were all indeed famous people, but then I asked them a question that stumped them.

"What problem did they solve? What purpose did they serve?" They could not answer.

I'm not dismissing the success, influence, and impact of the people they named, nor their value as human beings. But it was clear that my then nine-year-old son and thirteen-year-old daughter were conditioned to think that value is measured by fame and fortune, and could I blame them? After all, I believed the same at their age, and continued to until I was thirty-six. What happened at thirty-six, you might ask, that shifted my belief? I read Bob Buford's bestselling work *Halftime*.

Halftime has impacted my life and shaped my thought process more than any other book, second only to the Bible itself. In *Halftime*, Buford offers that this world conditions us for success but that we are created for significance. He suggests that no matter what level of success we achieve in life, sometime between the ages of thirty-five and fifty-five, we will recognize that something is missing, and many people misdiagnose this revelation as a midlife crisis. What is the thing that is missing? Purpose.

Before we get too far along in this chapter, I want to assure you that I am in no way demonizing success, and neither is Buford. In fact, he also suggests that you can be successful and miss out on a life of significance, but it's impossible to live a life of significance and not be successful.

Some of the most famous people who ever lived, those whom history has well and long remembered are those who led lives of significance, those whose purpose we can read about today, because of the impact they had on humanity. While traveling this past year in the UK, which I will share more about in a later chapter, I walked through different abbeys and castles and passed countless tombstones. Many of the names I didn't recognize—a lot of kings, queens, and nobility. I slowly strolled and read the engraved details of the reign and lineage of each, but stopped in my tracks when I found myself standing at the resting places in Westminster Abbey of Sir Issac Newton, most known for his theory on the law of gravity; Charles Dickens, one of the most recognized authors of all time; and Sir Roger Bannister, the English neurologist who broke the four-minute mile and challenged the believed limitations of the physiological performance of the human body. I have no idea how much money they made, how many followers they had, or how famous they were in their time, but I did know that their tombstones needed no explanation. In fact, each one only had their name and years of life engraved, with no other details required.

Some believe success and fame come from our upbringing, from the good fortune of the families we are born into, or perhaps simply the result of luck. I'll say it again: our circumstances don't define us, but our choices do. Sometimes we need someone to step into our lives to simply show us our potential; other times we need to ask if our circumstances are happening to us or for us and use them as inspiration to help us realize our purpose.

Sir Issac Newton came from a family of farmers and he never knew his father who died three months before he was born. His father was an uneducated man who could not sign his own name. Issac's early school reports described him as "idle" and "inattentive," but his uncle saw great promise in him and prepared him for university. The rest is history.

Charles Dickens's father was imprisoned for debt, and as a result, Charles had to be withdrawn from school to perform manual work in a factory. His childhood struggles would provide great perspective and be the inspiration behind his now-enshrined writing career and legendary works of literature from *Great Expectations* to *A Christmas Carol*.

Sir Roger Bannister was born into a working-class family. He took an early interest in running after his father won three junior cross-country cup championships at City of Bath Boys' School, but then their home was severely damaged in the WWII bombing raid of Bath, and the family moved to London. His childhood experiences both gave him great resilience to pursue becoming an Olympic athlete. His running career was tattered with defeat, and the Olympic medal eluded him as he finished fourth in the 1952 games. He spent two months debating on giving up running, but Bannister would ultimately set a new goal to break the four-minute mile and would do so in 1954, earning him recognition as the fastest man in history.

You could label Bannister's great achievement as success, but more important than the record he achieved is the significance behind his accomplishment. Prior to Bannister running what became known as the sub-four-minute mile, it was widely believed in the scientific world that the human body could not survive such a run, with thoughts that the human heart would explode in the process. And because science said it couldn't be done, few tried. Since that belief was proved false, over 1,755 athletes have broken the "four-minute barrier" and countless more have achieved other levels of significance that were once not thought possible because of Bannister's inspiring determination. His name alone has become known globally as an inspiration to challenge the status quo.

If only we would chase our purpose with the same level of determination that Bannister chased breaking the four-minute mile barrier. What would we unlock for humanity? What would we unlock for ourselves?

The problem is we spend too much time chasing the wrong things in life and often find out when it is too late. This is common in the business world. I have met too many CEOs who were successful at work but failing at home, and if you asked them, in life in general.

"We spend too much time chasing the wrong things in life and often find out when it is too late."

Perhaps nowhere is this better captured than in what is known to be the last interview with Steve Jobs, whose life's work revolutionized the world and then was ended by cancer at the young age of fifty-six. Jobs is recorded as saying these words in his final days:

"I reached the pinnacle of success in the business world. In others' eyes, my life is an epitome of success. However, aside from work, I have little joy. In the end, wealth is only a fact of life that I am accustomed to. At this moment, lying on the sick bed and recalling my whole life, I realize that all the recognition and wealth that I took so much pride in, have paled and become meaningless in the face of impending death."

You can employ someone to drive the car for you, make money for you, but you cannot have someone to bear the sickness for you. Material things lost can be found. But there is one thing that can never be found when it is lost: life.

I have read this many times, and often every time with great sadness in my heart for Jobs. To think that he will forever be known as the man who founded Apple, invented the Mac, the iPhone, take your pick, had all the money, fame, and success in the world, but wished he had more time with the everyday people in his life. And if it were not for this interview, the world might remember little of his significance as a person, as a human being. To me, his insightful final words are a far greater gift to the future of humanity than any of the inventions he has left us with—we can learn much from them. While success is a lifelong pursuit, significance is found in every moment that we are present. This is where true purpose lives and what Jobs is calling us to. Don't miss the moments of significance in your pursuit of success.

We can lose our identity in our accomplishments. I recently have been captivated by how our natural inclination when we meet another person for the first time is to ask them what they do. Their response is also a title followed by the organization they are associated with. And sadly, we often tend to start sizing each other up depending on what that title or organization is. Society has equated identity with title and accomplishments for centuries, and we continue to perpetuate that today. But what if we chose not to?

What if instead of asking, "What do you do?" we chose to ask, "What do you like to do?"

What if we chose to begin by seeing people for who they are and how they would choose to spend their time rather than how they have to spend their time?

For those who truly love their profession, the answer may be the same, but for years various studies have proven that around 83 percent of people globally are actively disengaged in the work that they do, and that number has barely moved a few percentage points in the last few decades. This would suggest that most people are not spending their time in a way that engages or fulfills them; I would suggest that they are not finding purpose in their work.

I've shared before that purpose is composed of four things: what we are good at, what the world needs, what we love to do, and what we get paid to do. Yet when we ask others what they do, they typically respond with what they get paid to do.

But perhaps if we asked people what they like to do, they might reveal not just what they like to do, but also what they are good at, or even a need in the world they are passionate about serving. By inserting those two simple words "like to" in that sentence, we can unlock the whole person and learn more about them, which would lead to more organic and purposeful dialogue rather than the same old small talk.

I challenge you from this moment forward to stop asking people what they do and the next time you meet someone new, ask them what they like to do and see how they respond. It will feel awkward, they might feel awkward, they might even ask you what you mean, but the conversation will start much richer and deeper and will ultimately flow more naturally.

This is an exercise I use a lot when working with leaders to help individuals in their organizations understand how to help their people find purpose at work. It's always so fulfilling to sit back and watch as titles get laid down and people connect on a human level and learn new things about each other. One thing I see happen a lot is how often a leader realizes a set of skills that a person in their charge is not using in their role, and they are reassigned to a role where they can use those skills. In those instances, three things immediately occur. First, that person immediately becomes engaged. Second, their performance significantly improves. Third, a company need is met. And the result of all three of those together? The individual finds purpose, meaning, and significance in their work, and success for both the individual and the company follows.

Earlier, I mentioned the character Max from the hospital TV drama *New Amsterdam*. There is one episode that I love where Max runs an experiment matching people's skill sets to the needs of the hospital.

At one point, Max meets a technician who has been sitting in the basement of the hospital and had not seen a patient in eight years because of new technology that made his former methodology antiquated. Max goes into the basement and as soon as he sees him, he puts down a book he is casually reading and fearfully asks, "Am I about to get fired?"

Max calms him down and asks, "Do you like your job?"

The X-ray tech replies, "I used to. I loved it, actually. Everybody needed me. Docs used to say nobody handled radiograph paper better than I did."

Max then reintroduces himself: "I'm Max Goodwin, I'm the medical director here. I'd like to find you a new job. A job that makes you feel needed again. Would you be interested?"

Imagine a world where every leader, in every position, in every industry was like Max. Imagine if we didn't just give people jobs, but we gave people jobs that gave them significance because the role activated their purpose. But we continue to miss reaping the beautiful benefits of Max's experiment because leaders tend to be far more focused on success than significance.

The good news is that if you are a leader, you can decide to be like Max. And if you are an individual contributor, you don't need to wait for permission to align the work that you like to do with where you see a need around you to do it.

For some of us, we need an unexpected life event to happen before we wake up to the insights that I am sharing with you. I mentioned early Bob Buford's book *Halftime* but I didn't tell you why I read it. The truth is a good friend gave me that book with a disclosure, "If you read this book, you might question your life choices." Because of that statement, *Halftime* sat on my desk for six months, until one rainy day when I was driving our daughter Vera to school in the morning. It was our normal short drive, about fifteen minutes from our home. We often enjoyed singing in the car together to her favorite songs. This morning, as we pulled up to the school, I turned my left turn signal on, stopped and sang with her as we waited for oncoming traffic to pass. Our singing suddenly turned into screaming as a car behind us who was not paying attention had not recognized we had stopped and slammed into us at fifty miles an hour. Our car was crushed from the back all the way up to my daughter's car seat—which saved her life. I flew forward with my seat belt on, hit the steering wheel, bounced back, and hit my chair so hard it broke, and I found myself horizontal with my head in the back seat area, staring my baby girl screaming with one thought in my mind: *I have to get her out of the car.* That was my only purpose in that moment. Nothing else mattered. I couldn't move, but thankfully the crash was so loud that people inside our church, which was attached to her school, came to the scene and got her out of the car. I went to the hospital, where I laid in a neck brace for hours with a lot of time to reflect about what mattered in life.

Before this moment, I was chasing success; my ladder was against the wrong wall, and I knew it. But none of that mattered now. I questioned, what if I couldn't walk again, what if I couldn't write again, what if I couldn't walk Vera down the aisle one day, what if I couldn't hold her again? Two sets of questions that both involved the mobile capability of my hands and feet, but what was clear to me was that it was more important that I got to have a second chance to use them to fulfill my purpose as her father than in the pursuit of my ambitions. I thank God every day for that second chance.

Some of us learn from such traumatic life experiences, and sadly some fall back into old patterns. I recently read an article entitled "Wake Up Grateful" by Kristi Nelson, who was diagnosed with stage four Hodgkin's Lymphoma at age thirty-three. In the article, she shared these words:

"Not sure how much more time was mine, I was awestruck by every moment, every person, and every thing. Being grateful the first few years was relatively easy and revelatory. I would wake up in a room bathed in light, hear birds singing, and notice I was still breathing... I could put both feet on the floor and walk freely to a kitchen where I could make a cup of tea. It was enough to make me start each day with tears of joy. Being alive was enough.

"But over time, all those amazing reasons to feel grateful joined the ranks of the taken-for-granted. I got healthy and busy. I began chasing goals and the fulfillment they promised. I martyred myself to a job, complained about things like traffic, my weight, and colds. I ruthlessly compared myself to others, succumbed to retail therapy and debt, and suffered from stress. Each year that passed, I built up a kind of gratitude tolerance—what used to be enough got left in the dust in the pursuit of having more. Having cheated death, I began cheating life."

That last sentence convicts me so deeply. *"Having cheated death, I began cheating life."* How many of us are currently cheating life, without having had to have cheated death? Don't allow your focus on success to rob you of experiencing the full significance of life, which is found by focusing not on what you need to do in each moment, but rather on who you need to be in each moment.

You don't need to be all things to all people; you just need to be all of you to the person right in front of you. When you do that intentionally and consistently in each moment, you will find yourself living a life of significance, fulfilling your purpose, and success in its truest and most important form will follow.

Four Thoughts to Overcome the Thief of Success

1. Review how you spend your time and energy and what
    you are focused on most of the time. What are you in
    pursuit of? Are you constantly chasing a goal, a number, an
    accomplishment? Those aren't bad things, but ask yourself
    what moments of significance you have missed because you
    were too focused on those ambitions.

2. What problems are you solving or what difference are you
    making in the work that you do? When was the last time
    you wrote down the impact you made at the end of the day?
    I challenge you for one week to place a notepad and a pen
    next to your bed and each night write down the name of one
    person you impacted each day and how you impacted them.

3. Write down what success looks like to you. Then write down
    what significance looks like to you. Are they the same?
    Where, if at all, do they overlap? The overlap is the purpose
    you should be living in.

4. I encourage you to read *Halftime* by Bob Buford. It's a
    tremendous book that will challenge you to shift your mindset
    from pursuing a life of success to living a life of significance
    and purpose, and in addition to experiencing fulfillment,
    success will find you.

Thief #11
INDIFFERENCE

"The only thing necessary for the triumph of evil is for good men to do nothing."

—Formerly attributed to Edmund Burke

I woke up at 4:30 a.m., quickly got dressed, jumped in the car, and took the all-too-familiar, hour-long drive to Detroit Metro Airport to catch a 6:30 flight to New York City. I had barely slept the night before as the anticipation of seeing my dear friends and colleagues Garry Ridge and Andy Brooks, and our long-awaited meeting with the developers of Heartcount was just hours away. News had rolled in that a major winter storm was about to hit New York at the same time as our arrival and to anticipate travel delays. As I drove closer to the airport, I kept checking my flight status, which was on time, until the moment that I pulled into the parking garage. All I could think about was how much longer I could have slept as I stared at my phone notification that my flight was delayed three hours.

As I passed through security, with plenty of time on my hands to now repurpose, my delayed flight status changed again. This time, the notification read "Canceled." Delta kindly rebooked me on a three p.m. flight to LaGuardia, which happened to be the same time as our meeting. I was suddenly faced with a choice: sit in the terminal for eight hours, fly to New York, miss the meeting, and catch the footnotes at dinner, or send my regrets for not attending and head home. I went to the Delta counter to determine the likelihood that the three p.m. flight would take off, given the weather conditions battering the Northeast. I was second in line, with a couple and their infant booked on the same flight in front of me. To my surprise, they got rebooked on a ten a.m. flight to LaGuardia, and I humorously but also seriously shouted from behind them, "Please make that three!" Thankfully, I was given the last seat on that flight.

When I arrived at my seat, a middle seat (which I rarely choose), I engaged two other gentlemen in my row, motioning to my seat in between them, thanked them for getting up to let me in, and then started the same informal discussions that many of us do on a plane. Are you heading home or is this home? Business or personal trip? Usual small talk. But before I could say much, the gentleman to my right, whose name was Brian, shared that he too was on the same original canceled flight. We shared a brief conversation on how well Delta had handled the situation. What began as all talk turned into one the most delightful conversations I have had on a plane, and it lasted for the entire flight. We shared about our families, and Brian shared about his son. When Brian learned through our conversation about my first book, *Finding Purpose at Work*, he quickly took an interest in the subject and wanted to get a copy of the book for his son. As we continued our conversation, I sat in awe of the timing of our meeting each other, as I learned that what his son was currently walking through in life coincided specifically with the insights that I had offered in that work. Before I took notice, Brian had already purchased a copy of the book, but I happened to have a copy in my bag to give him personally. He continued to express his gratitude for our paths crossing and for how my words might impact his son. I shared my immense gratitude for meeting him and for the opportunity to potentially make an impact.

Imagine if we had not engaged in conversation. That moment
and impact would have been lost. Far too many of us walk around
indifferent to the fact that there is purpose at work in every moment
if we choose to engage. As I have shared, I don't get this right all
the time. There are plenty of flights that I have been on where I
have sat next to a stranger for a couple of hours and barely said
hello, and I often wonder what purpose was lost in those moments.
Perhaps a new relationship? Perhaps some collaborative impact?
Or perhaps nothing at all. I will never know, but I do know in each
of those moments, indifference prevented me from engaging in
conversation. But many of us were brought up this way, told at an
early age to "mind our own business." Indifference is part of our
human conditioning.

> *"Far too many of us walk around indifferent to the fact that there
> is purpose at work in every moment if we choose to engage in
> the moment."*

One of my favorite flight stories is one I heard recently at a
conference. Chad Spencer, one of the speakers at the conference,
shared in his talk how he was on a plane and happened to sit
right behind Chris Tomlin. If you are unfamiliar with Chris, he is a
Grammy Award-winning singer-songwriter widely known across
the contemporary Christian community. Chad knew of Chris, but
did not know Chris, and Chris certainly did not know Chad. But
seizing the moment, Chad decided to pull up one of Chris's songs
on his phone, reached around Chris's chair and put his headphones
in his ear. Chris, startled, turned around and looked at Chad, and
Chad humorously said to him, "You know this guy? His music
stinks!" Laughing, Chad said, "I knew right there we were either
about to throw down or become best friends." Chad and Chris
ended up talking the rest of the flight together. Chad owned and
operated many furniture stores in the US, and one of the charities
they had started was called Angel Armies, which at the time
supported over thirteen thousand families and thirty-five thousand

kids. Chris offered to support Chad's mission, and in doing so wrote a song entitled "Angel Armies," also known as "Whom Shall I Fear," which earned the number one spot on Billboard charts in 2013, reaching and impacting millions of people worldwide. Imagine if Chad had chosen to simply "mind his own business."

Many of us were brought up this way, told at an early age to "mind our own business." Indifference is part of our human conditioning, and sadly it has not just led to lost moments of purpose and impact, but historically to great human tragedy. Amy and I were recently in London where I had been invited to speak at the Global Workplace Innovation Summit. Since it was our first time in the United Kingdom together, we decided to spend ten days together exploring all that London had to offer, and eventually made our way to Scotland to meet friends. While in London, we visited every historical site of significance within walking distance of the subway system, known there as "the Tube." As we traveled from station to station, a voice kept coming over the speaker, announcing, "If you see something, say something, we'll sort it. See it. Say it. Sorted." It was a constant call to action to not be indifferent to any potential activity around us that was threatening to another person.

As I read the signs around the trains and the stations, I noticed a common theme of various calls to action to be present and aware of our surroundings in the moment, as well as the well-being of those around us. From the famous signs that read "Mind the gap" so that we did not trip or fall over each other in the rush to get in and out of the train cars, to subtle signs in the trains directing us to give up our seats to those who might need it more than us, such as those with child or a limited walking ability. Despite how busy people were in London, indifference seemed absent. The people we engaged with, while focused on where they were going, were also somehow present. On multiple occasions, I even received a tap on the shoulder from a stranger to let me know that the zipper on my bag was open, a courteous reminder to close it and to be aware of the threat of potential pickpockets in the area who could take advantage of us as tourists. I've traveled to many of the busiest cities in the states, from New York to Los Angeles, Chicago to Atlanta, and I have not previously come across such a level of awareness and common courtesy toward others.

Much of this culture in London I imagine comes from its extensive history of learning from the consequences of indifference. While reading about Winston Churchill, one of the most remembered and memorialized leaders in England's history, I learned that prior to becoming prime minister, Churchill provided many early warnings to his government about the danger of Hitler's growing influence and intentions in the late 1930s. The word used to describe England's and the rest of Europe's lack of response to Churchill's early warnings was *indifference*. As I continued reading, I could not help being overcome by thinking of how history might have been different, how the tragedy of the Holocaust could have been prevented, how many millions of lives would not have been taken by such evil or lost in war.

I have often quoted Edmund Burke, who was once thought to have said, "The only thing necessary for the triumph of evil is for good men to do nothing." This popular quote is used to warn against the dangers of complacency. Unfortunately, research suggests, Burke never said these words, but rather said, *"When bad men combine, the good must associate, else they will fail, one by one, an unpitied sacrifice in a contemptible struggle."* This became the inspiration for John Stuart Mill a century later when he said, *"Bad men need nothing more to compass their ends than that good men should look on and do nothing."*

No matter who said what, all three statements provide the same message: Evil will triumph in the face of indifference and complacency.

COMPLACENCY

Complacency can be an underlining cause of indifference, and so I present to you another subchapter. A while back in my former career I had a colleague who was famous for saying, "It is what it is." Those words were like nails on a chalkboard for me. I translated them in my mind to "I don't care enough to do something about the situation." Granted, sometimes circumstances are out of our control, but our attitudes and choices are always within our control. We can choose to have a defeated mindset and let our circumstances dictate our reality, or we can choose to view such moments as an invitation to be a catalyst for change, to step into purpose.

In his blog, *Leader Influence*, Dennis Baker addressed my thoughts and sentiments perfectly. He stated:

"The phrase 'it is what it is' becomes the motto for many people who allow complacency to embed their lives and way of thinking. In fact, that phrase indicates complacency has overtaken their ability to transform their results. Complacency is like a deadly virus dormant in your system. It is lurking to kill your goals, dreams, and success. It has the power to rob you blind of new experience, positive change, and personal growth. The worst thing about complacency is the infected person is usually unaware that he or she is at risk. Complacency occurs in all of us. It is present in our personal lives and careers."

I would also add that it is present in most organizations. One of my favorite quotes when it comes to organizational complacency is, "The seven words of every dying organization are 'We have always done things this way.' " I believe that can be applied on an individual level as well. Few of us welcome change and even fewer have the conviction to be a catalyst for change. Yet every worthwhile invention, system, or resource we have today was birthed from someone who saw a purpose and chose not to be complacent.

Here are three suggestions from that same article on how to confront complacency.

Be Curious. Without a curious mind and curious heart, we become stagnant in our thoughts and ideas. This allows complacency to become our comfort place. John Maxwell said, "When you lack curiosity, you breed indifference."

We just spoke at length about indifference. Curiosity, on the other hand, promotes change and a desire to always improve. Curiosity requires wisdom and courage, like the explorers who first set off around the globe. When you are in exploration mode, you may be moving forward or side-to-side, but you never go backward. You put yourself in a position to create influence rather than falling into the traps of complacency.

I love what my friend Nick Craig, author of *Leading From Purpose*, said at Purpose Summit 2024: "The key to living out our purpose is to not just follow the maps of those who came before us, but to become the map makers for those who are yet to come."

Challenge the Status Quo. As complacency sets in, our ability to think differently is minimized by our inability to process anything other than what we already know. Instead of seeing the opportunity to move forward, we wait to seek permission and find ourselves passed up by great opportunities.

I'll never forget the words of my friend Dennis Moseley Williams, who said at the first Purpose Summit in 2019, "Your purpose does not need permission. There is the work that's assigned, and there is the work that is required. Stop waiting for permission to solve the problem you know needs to be solved."

Keep hope alive at all costs. Regardless of life or business situations, hope will always shine a positive light. Hope is the belief that circumstances in the future will be better. It's not a wish that things will get better but an actual belief, even when there may be no evidence to support it. Remember the words of Dr. Martin Luther King Jr., who said, "You don't have to see the whole staircase, just take the first step."

One of my favorite references over time has been the concept of the dash, the short punctuation mark that sits between our first and last day on this earth—it represents so much. My recent time in London gave me much pause to think about my dash. I visited the resting places of people—some names well-known, some not—who lived hundreds of years before us and took note of the differences in which they were memorialized. What is interesting is that the size of their memorial was directly proportionate to their significance, which is contrary to our modern era's emphasis on success. The significance of the dashes of those memorialized in the past was not representative of what they had attained for themselves but the difference they had made while here. The purpose they had served. The reason their lives mattered to the world.

There is a poem entitled "The Dash" by Linda Ellis. I encourage you to look up and read the whole poem, there is a particular stanza that powerfully points out the most overlooked part of every tombstone. It reads:

I read of a man who stood to speak
At the funeral of a friend
He referred to the dates on the tombstone
From the beginning...to the end

He noted that first came the date of birth
And spoke the following date with tears,
But he said what mattered most of all
Was the dash between those years

Stepping fully into your purpose will require you to get intentional about your dash.

It will implore you to challenge and test your convictions.

It will demand that you rid yourself of indifference and complacency.

Are you up for the challenge?

If not, then I implore you, what are your convictions?

Do you have any? What is the deepest problem or pain you see in the world that you want to change or solve? What can you do about it? What will you do about it?

Are you sitting on a tack? Remember the dog barking back in the chapter on excuses? How bad does the pain need to be before you choose to get up?

Benjamin Disraeli, former prime minister of the United Kingdom, once said, "I have brought myself, by long meditation, to the conviction that a human being with a settled purpose must accomplish it, and that nothing can resist a will stake even existence upon its fulfillment."

Notice he included "by long meditation." I warned you early on that this was not meant to be a feel-good book, but rather a work to challenge you to think long and hard about the reason for your

being, and if you have made it this far, then you are doing just
that. So, take another moment and revisit these last few pages.
Write down your convictions. Place them where you will regularly
be reminded of them and resolve to wake up every day to do
something about them. Your dash is being written at this moment.

Four Thoughts to Overcome the Thieves of Indifference and Complacency

1. Recognize that you matter and that you can make a
    difference. We often look at historical figures who did
    something to shape the world and distance ourselves from
    them, but the reality is they were all people just like you and
    me at some point. The only thing that makes them different is
    that they acted on their convictions.

2. What are your convictions? Reflect on the deepest problem
    or pain point in the world that you want to see solved, and
    ask yourself what you can do about it. Even if it is the smallest
    action. Small actions can lead to tremendous impact, and
    that impact may just be a decision away.

3. Be present in every moment. Recognize that the immediate
    needs of those around us may be invitations to step into our
    purpose in those moments, and sometimes, you might need
    to get uncomfortable with engaging someone sitting right
    next to you to discover that need.

4. Think of your dash. What will it represent? No matter what
    you have or have not achieved yet, remain curious, challenge
    the status quo, and if you are already fighting a good fight,
    stay steadfast and keep hope alive at all costs.

Thief #12

UNBELIEF

"It always seems impossible until it's done."
—Nelson Mandela

"What if?" By now you know that these two words consume me.
In fact, I ended up choosing those two simple but powerful words
to be the title of the talk I gave at the fifth anniversary of The
Purpose Summit in Charlotte, North Carolina. They also became
the guiding words of this past year as I processed some major
decisions personally and professionally, including potentially
moving our family to Charlotte. Our pros and cons list on that move
was filled with a bunch of "what ifs," both positive and negative.
We were filled with the excitement of new possibilities, adventures,
memories, and opportunities, and we felt a strong pull guided
by our strong faith. We were also gripped with fear—fear of the
unknown, unfamiliar, uncertain, and unseen. But perhaps we were
really struggling with unbelief.

More dreams have been left unrealized, goals left unaccomplished,
potential left unreached, and purpose left unfulfilled than we can
possibly quantify because of unbelief. But what if?

What if you believed in what you are being called to, what you are
capable of, what you were meant to experience, what you were
meant to do, and who you were meant to be?

The truth is, we have all asked ourselves "what if" either consciously or subconsciously at some point, and for some, it's a daily question. But it's a question that far too many can answer with what they currently can see instead of what they can envision, and dare I say, believe.

I recently was on a call with my friend and fellow MG100 coach, Stephanie Broaders, discussing the move to Charlotte, where she and her family had also moved to and now call home. During our call she shared these words with me from the late Myles Monroe: "Davin, do you know the difference between sight and vision?" She continued, "Sight is what you can see. Vision is what will come to pass, despite what you see." Simple, you might say, but profound. These words arrested both my mind and my heart the moment she said them.

She didn't know that another friend of mine, Dr. Amber Selling, whom I mentioned earlier, had hosted a podcast dedicated to her newborn baby girl, Elleanna Belle, and in it, she assigned a letter and word of the alphabet to a different person in her thought-leader circle, and she assigned me "V" for *vision*. I flew down to Charlotte for a speaking engagement and while there and recorded a video focused on vision, while standing on top of the dugout of Truist Field with the Charlotte skyline behind me. Initially my message would be focused on the vision we had to bring The Purpose Summit to Charlotte, but while speaking, my mind was thrust back into a memory from fifteen years prior of a vision that I was given.

In 2007, Amy and I celebrated our first year of marriage and took a road trip from Michigan to Myrtle Beach, South Carolina. The trip was initially for business purposes. We were newlyweds on a tight budget and couldn't afford the airfare for both of us to go, so we carpooled with another couple. We stopped in Charlotte for dinner and stayed the night and continued the trip the next morning. I'll

never forget this moment—the memory is so crisp, so vivid, so
tangible, as if I can reach back in time and touch it. There we stood,
waiting for a table outside of an old firehouse-turned-pizzeria, and I
was captivated by the simple but magnificent sight of the Charlotte
skyline above my head, and below a cloudless sunny sky. My eyes
were fixed specifically on the tallest tower, nicknamed the "Taj
McColl" after Hugh McColl, former CEO of NationsBank, which
eventually became Bank of America. The tower, with its unique
illuminated crown-shaped top symbolizing the "Queen City," still
dominates the Charlotte skyline, drawing attention from miles
around. That evening, I peered out my hotel window, and almost
audibly, I could hear, "Davin, one day, you and your family will call
this place home." We didn't even have kids yet, but I could envision
us living in this place, something that I had not been able to do
anywhere else other than in Philly, my hometown.

It's important to understand the significance of my obsession with
this skyline. Growing up in Philadelphia, I was always enamored by
the Philly skyline as I watched it grow over the first eighteen years
of my life living there. When I was born, the tallest building was
city hall, known for the statue of William Penn, which sits atop its
tower, and which was used as the height limit for any building that
was to be built in the city, until 1987 when One Liberty Place was
constructed and became my new obsession. My obsession with the
Philly skyline was conflicting as a diehard Philly sports fan, for there
was a belief that no Philly team would ever win a championship
now that a building taller than the statue of William Penn had
been built. It became known as the "Curse of Billy Penn." I never
believed in that curse, but, like every Philly native, experienced
the heartache of an inexplicable twenty-one-year professional
sports championship drought until the Phillies won the World
Series in 2008.

I have traveled to many cities in my life with far more impressive and expanding skylines than the Philly skyline, but none of them ever moved me emotionally, and none of them ever felt like home, except for the brief vision that I was given in Charlotte.

That vision was filed back into my mind when we left the next morning for Myrtle Beach, and I had not returned to Charlotte until June 2023, when we began the site selection process for Purpose Summit 2024. I made four trips to the Queen City over the next five months, and it was on my final trip of 2023 that I found myself speaking at Truist Field with the Bank of America tower behind me. While speaking, I also heard, "Davin, remember that vision from fifteen years ago? Get your family ready."

Did I really hear what I just heard? What if that vision was real? The real question I had to ask myself was, what did I believe?

At that moment, I decided to shift my talk title to "What do you believe?" These were the questions I asked the audience that day, and I invite you to pause and ask yourself the same questions:

What, or where, do you believe you are being called to?
What do you believe you are capable of?
What do you believe you are meant to do?
What purpose do you believe you were created for?

Perhaps you have never had a moment as tangible and audible as I experienced, but don't use that as an excuse. We have covered excuses at length already, and I'll remind you that an excuse is a reason stuffed with a lie, and I would offer that the real reason most people don't experience the fullness of purpose in their life is the result of unbelief.

There is an old story about a lion held in captivity by only a cheesecloth. The lion was originally placed in a large iron cage with its food set on one end and a place for it to sleep set on the opposite end. Each day the lion would walk in circles around the cage, roaring fervently, looking for a way to escape its four-walled iron-barred cage. Then a cheesecloth was placed over the top of the cage, blocking the lion's vision from anything beyond what it could see within the confines of its small habitat. Eventually the lion's roar grew silent and it paced between where it slept and where it ate. One day, the bars were removed from the cage, with only the cheesecloth standing between the lion and its freedom. But the lion couldn't see beyond the cheesecloth, so it never stepped out of its perceived captivity.

Many of us have been that lion, living life only within the confines of what we can see, with no vision beyond our current circumstances. The roar that was once within us to explore all that we believed was possible for our lives grows silent, and so does our purpose, as we choose to stay in the captivity of our unbelief.

 "The real reason most people don't experience the fullness of purpose in their life is the result of unbelief."

All too often we only allow what we can see to dictate what it is we believe. But that defeats the entire premise of belief. Believing is knowing without seeing. My friend Joe Colavito is good at giving new meaning and perspective to words. In a recent conversation we discussed the meaning of the word *division*. The standard meaning of the word is to "separate something into parts."

Incredibly, if we separate the word itself into two parts, "di-vision," we can redefine it as "two different visions," or not looking at the same vision. Looking only at what we can see right in front of us and not beyond our circumstances into what is possible.

You might not be moving toward your vision because you may be divided between what you currently see and the vision of what is possible for you.

I never saw myself as an author, or a speaker, for that matter. While I had admired and studied many authors and speakers from afar for almost two decades, I never thought becoming either was possible for me. It wasn't until I gave a talk in 2012 for CVS Health as an employee of the company that another colleague came up to me after the talk and said, "How did you do that?"

I replied, "How did I do what?"

He said, "Give that incredible talk on the fly, with no preparation?"

I said, "I simply went up there and spoke about what I knew, passionately and with great conviction, because I want people to do something with what I had to share with them."

He was the first person to ever say to me, "You are a very inspiring speaker, and you should do more of that." It took someone else seeing something in me that I didn't see in myself for me to believe it, and to cast a vision of what I could become. We both moved on from CVS Health, and he eventually became the first person to hire me to give a talk to his employees at PetSmart. That became the official start of my speaking career.

When it came to books, I loved reading and used my social media platforms to highlight the works of so many great authors to share their impact. Eventually I started to write articles about many of their works, and then started writing articles about my journey and gleaned insights along the way. Those articles gained a lot of traction on social media and eventually showed up in various publications. Several people had reached out to me and suggested that I write a book, but again, I couldn't envision myself as a published author. I started to ask myself, "What if?" and began work on a manuscript. Then something incredible happened.

In fall 2019, my wife Amy and I were invited to attend a conference in Boca Raton, Florida. We had accepted the invitation, and two days prior, she came down with pneumonia. We sent our regrets that we could not attend. Fortunately, the same conference was going to take place in February 2020 in Laguna Beach, California, and they invited us to attend then. I happened to have a client in Orange County whom I had previously come in to speak for and thought I would reach out to let him know that I would be in town and see if he wanted to grab dinner. When he found out I was coming, he asked if I could come in a day earlier to speak at another event he was hosting. Happily, I changed my flights to do so, and the next day he called me back and asked how long I would be on the West Coast. When I said just until February 28, he asked if while I in the area I could speak at a symposium in Lake Tahoe on March 4 as well. Again, I happily agreed and changed my flights. I now had talks scheduled from February 26–March 4 in Laguna Beach, Costa Mesa, and Lake Tahoe with my only free days being March 1–3. I decided I would stay in Laguna Beach for those three days and use that time as a writing retreat to work on my manuscript. I then got a call from the Ken Blanchard Companies, whose work I had been certified to teach, and they asked if I could come to their annual conference. I asked when the conference was, and you guessed it—March 1–3, and guess where it was being held? San Diego. I decided to change my itinerary once again, forgo my writing retreat, and planned to attend the Ken Blanchard conference on the first and second before flying to Lake Tahoe on the third. When I arrived in San Diego, I was met with such joy by the team there. Michelle Shone, who had been my contact at Blanchard, greeted me and said, "Davin, we are so glad you could make it!"

I said, "Michelle, it is my honor to be here. Ken has poured so much into my life through his work. I'm grateful to be able to give something back."

She said, "Well, have you ever met Ken?"

When I told her I hadn't, she said, "Well, he just walked in right behind you!"

I turned around, looked at Ken, who had been my mentor of two decades through the reading of his books, and said, "Ken, it's an honor, I've waited twenty years to meet you."

He told me, "Well, I won't hold that against you, young man. Tell me, have you gotten any eggs yet?"

"Eggs?" I asked.

He said, "Breakfast. Have you had breakfast?"

I said, "No, sir, I have not."

He said, "Let's go have some eggs."

We walked into the hotel and made our way to a round table, where we enjoyed our eggs and talked for an hour. He continued to ask me about my work, truly embodying the servant leader I knew him to be, always curious about others. He then said, "Tell me, young man, have you written anything on this purpose stuff yet?"

I said, "You know, Ken, I was actually supposed to be working on a manuscript today and tomorrow but have put that off to be here with you."

He said, "What you have to say is really important, and people need to hear it. When you finish that manuscript, would you please send it to me? I would like to write the foreword to that book."

My jaw dropped, and I began texting Amy under the table, letting her know that Ken Blanchard, my leadership mentor whom I had never met, had just encouraged me to finish a book and offered to write the foreword to it.

Ken and I spent the rest of the day together and when we had finished dinner, he got up to excuse himself for the evening. I thanked him for such a memorable day, and once again for his life's work. He started to make his way toward the door, walking with his cane, and then came to a pause. He turned, pointed his cane at me, and said, "Now you better get writing, young man; I'm not getting any younger."

I returned home from my West Coast travels on March 6, 2020. Only days later, the world shut down to COVID, and as I shared earlier, I went into my basement and finished my first book, *Finding Purpose at Work*. I never imagined that companies would end up purchasing hundreds of copies of that book for their people and that it would propel my writing and speaking career. It's not lost on me all the small events that had to come together for that to happen.

I share this story with you in such great detail for a purpose. Do you remember when I told you that I wanted to quit? Well, I didn't tell you what happened just before Purpose Summit 2024, how it almost all fell apart and didn't happen. While we had 456 people registered, unfortunately, we were short of our budgeted goal to meet our expenses. Thankfully, we had a business line of credit to fall back on in case that were to happen. I logged into our account to draw from our available balance, and much to my surprise, received an email asking what the fund request was for. The bank had changed its policy to now review and approve every draw. I shared with them that it was to cover our expense gap for our event, and shortly after the call, I received an email that our draw was declined and our account was suspended. I now had just two days to come up with a significant sum of cash to pay the catering bill for the summit, and I was in a panic. I sat on the floor in our office in disbelief, lacking the strength or sight to take another step.

That same day, my dear friend Roger Norberg popped into our office, and said, "I was in the neighborhood and felt that I needed to stop by—you look like you can use a hug." Boy, did I ever.

I shared with him what had happened, and he asked if he could send a prayer request out to our C12 Forum group, and of course, I said, "Please do!"

In the meantime, our team continued to work on final details for the summit. I sat at our conference table with Lisa, while our chief experience officer was printing last-minute name badges, and our friend Adam Ritchie was setting up the online bookstore for all of the authors presenting at the summit.

Just then, I received a text message from my CPA, friend, and fellow C12 member, John Sanchez. He had read Roger's prayer request and asked me to call him ASAP.

I called John, and he said, "Davin, you won't believe this, but I am sitting here in the airport waiting with my son to board a flight to Atlanta for a fishing trip, and I read Roger's prayer request about your situation. I needed to call another client to follow up on a question he had, and I can't believe the timing of his question."

John called his client, whose name was Jim, and he said, "John, I am sitting on some cash, and I don't want to put it in the market, and the bank isn't giving me very much for it. Do you have any ideas on what I might be able to do with it?"

John shared with him that he had a friend whose bank had pulled his company line of credit, and he had this incredible leadership event that they needed funding for to pull off and suggested that he might want to step in and help.

Jim said, "Sounds like a great event and a good opportunity to help your friend out—have him give me a call."

I called Jim, such a delightful man. He was expecting my call, and we discussed the matter. He offered to provide a loan for the funds we needed, and we met at the bank the next afternoon. When I walked into the bank the next day, I looked around and saw a man much older than me—ninety-one years of age, to be specific— standing there with a cane and a smile on his face.

We greeted each other, took care of the matter, and then sat in the bank lobby for a while and talked. He asked, "Davin, you know a lot of businesspeople, why didn't you just ask someone for the money?"

I said, "Jim, I have never directly asked someone for money, but I believe that somehow God was going to provide a way as He always does, and for some reason, He chose you."

Jim said, "Why me?"

I replied, "Jim, I'm not sure; maybe there is some way I am supposed to help you or your family back, or perhaps I'm simply meant to share this story to help others with overcoming their unbelief during challenging circumstances." I continued, "In fact, I am finishing my second book right now, and I would like to include this story in the final chapter on unbelief if that is okay with you."

He said, "Well, that would be wonderful!"

We got up from the chairs in the bank lobby and started to make our way to the door. I thanked Jim again and then he stopped, pointed his cane at me, and said these exact words: "Now you better get writing, young man. I'm not getting any younger."

I stood there, frozen, remembering those same exact words Ken Blanchard had said to me four years prior when finishing my first book.

I then said, "Jim, I know why God chose you. Sit back down. I have a story to tell you."

I will forever be grateful that Jim came into my life when he did, not because he provided a check when we needed it most, but because he reaffirmed my belief when I needed it most.

We almost never know why things happen the way they do, especially in the most challenging of times. Sometimes we can't even see how to take the next step right in front of us. But that next step is always there. That step is belief.

I shared this work with my aunt Allison, prior to it being published, and she shared with me a powerful visual from her early years as a child riding horses. She said, "Davin, it's simple. The essence of overcoming your unbelief is your faith. As a rider, believing the horse will leap when it is directed to is faith. Similarly, the horse doesn't know what is on the other side of the fence, but it has faith that the rider can see what it cannot. You and your family had enough faith to take the leap."

Faith is believing in what you cannot see. Hebrews 11:1 says more specifically, "Faith is the realization of what is hoped for, and the evidence of things not seen."

Read that again: the "realization" and the "evidence." Those words are powerfully tangible. Whatever challenge you may be facing right now, even though you may not be able to see it, I want to encourage you that there is a purpose, and in time, that purpose will reveal itself, even if it is not on this side of heaven.

We started this discussion with the topic of comparison. We all have different circumstances we are facing, and likely vast levels of challenges that cannot fairly be compared to each other. Unwavering belief demonstrated by the likes of Horatio Spafford, Abraham Lincoln, and many others who have gone before us, has encouraged me in my most challenging times, helping me to find the strength to keep stepping forward, to keep believing there is a purpose, in all things.

It is my hope that the stories, struggles, and insights I have shared in this work will help you to face each of the thieves as they come to try and rob you of every purpose you are meant to step into moment by moment, so that you can fully become the person you were created to become, or perhaps like me, never even envisioned you could become.

It was once said, if you want to be remembered, do something worth writing about, or write something worth reading about.

I hope that because of this work you will step fully into your purpose in every area of your life, and that one day I might read about something significant you have done, or maybe even read something you have written.

May the words within these pages challenge you, inspire you, and equip you to believe, take action, and step into every purpose you were created for.

—Davin

Four Thoughts to Overcome the Thief of Unbelief

1. Recognize that everything we have was once thought impossible until it became a reality. Everything that has ever been invented or achieved is the result of overcoming unbelief, through challenging what is possible and believing, despite what may seem to be impossible.

2. Remember the words my friend Stephanie shared with me from the late Myles Monroe: "Do you know the difference between sight and vision? Sight is what you can see. Vision is what will come to pass, despite what you see."

3. Constantly ask yourself these questions, especially in the most challenging of circumstances:

    What, or where, do you believe you are being called to?

    What do you believe you are capable of?

    What do you believe you are meant to do?

    What purpose do you believe you were created for?

4. Wherever you may be in your faith or lack thereof, there is no shortage of evidence to prove that there are forces at work in our lives that we simply cannot explain. We call them coincidences. I choose to call them "Godincidences," recognizing that all things happen for a purpose beyond what we can see, imagine, or understand. Even in my darkest hours, my hold on that belief has propelled me to keep stepping into my purpose, day by day, moment by moment. Belief fuels hope. Hope inspires action. Action breeds purpose.

QUICK GUIDE TO IDENTIFYING THE 12 THIEVES OF PURPOSE

- **Comparison:** This thief occurs when individuals measure their self-worth and accomplishments against those of others, leading to feelings of inadequacy and dissatisfaction. Comparison can stifle personal growth and hinder the pursuit of one's unique purpose.

- **Competition:** Driven by the desire to outperform others, this thief can create unhealthy rivalry and pressure, preventing genuine collaboration and potentially damaging relationships.

- **Impatience:** This thief arises from the desire for immediate results or gratification, leading individuals to make hasty decisions and miss valuable opportunities for growth.

- **Distraction:** In a world filled with information and stimuli, distraction can make it difficult to maintain focus on one's goals and purpose. This thief can lead to a lack of progress and a feeling of being overwhelmed.

- **Excuses:** Blaming external factors or circumstances for one's lack of progress or success can prevent individuals from taking responsibility for their actions and growth. This thief stifles self-improvement and robs people of their dreams and reaching their full potential. Related to **procrastination:** The habit of putting off important tasks can result in missed opportunities and increased stress. This thief can significantly hinder personal and professional growth.

- **Fear:** This thief can paralyze individuals, preventing them from taking risks and pursuing their goals. Fear of failure, rejection, or change can limit personal growth and hinder the pursuit of one's purpose. Fear can lead to **doubt:** A lack of confidence or belief in one's abilities can lead to indecision and inaction. Doubt can prevent individuals from pursuing their dreams and reaching their full potential.

- **Lies:** Deceptive thoughts or beliefs about oneself, others, or the world can negatively impact decision-making and personal growth. This thief can lead to self-sabotage and prevent individuals from achieving their goals.

- **Guilt:** Excessive guilt over past mistakes or perceived shortcomings can hinder personal growth and lead to feelings of unworthiness.
  This thief prevents individuals from moving forward and embracing their full potential.

- **Quitting:** Giving up on one's goals or dreams too easily can result in a lack of perseverance and resilience. This thief robs individuals of the opportunity to learn from failure and grow stronger.

- **Success:** Ironically, achieving success can sometimes lead to complacency and a lack of motivation to continue growing. This thief can prevent individuals from pushing their boundaries and realizing their full potential.

- **Indifference:** A lack of interest or concern for personal growth, development, or purpose can result in a stagnant, unfulfilling life. This thief prevents individuals from embracing their unique potential and pursuing their dreams. Indifference can go hand-in-hand with **complacency:** A sense of contentment with one's current achievements or circumstances can lead to stagnation and a lack of growth. This thief prevents individuals from striving for continuous improvement and reaching their full potential.

- **Unbelief:** A lack of faith in oneself or a higher purpose can lead to feelings of aimlessness and despair. This thief can prevent individuals from embracing their potential and pursuing a meaningful, purpose-driven life.

WITH GRATITUDE

Thank you to my bride, Amy Salvagno, who provided the space, time, and support that I needed to write this book, and for being open to sharing vulnerable parts of our story to positively impact the lives of others. I am so grateful that I get to share this life with you and our kiddos.

Thank you to Scott Jeffrey Miller, my literary and speaking agent, who inspired me not to give up on this book, and to our publishing team who helped it get across the finish line. This book would not exist without your support and partnership.

Thank you to so many friends and colleagues who cheered me on along the way—you know who you are. Your encouragement and support helped me overcome each of these thieves personally in the very course of writing about them.

Thank you to my family for your unconditional love and support and your many prayers and messages of excitement in anticipation of this book becoming a reality.

And finally, and most importantly, I thank God and give Him all the glory for any impact that comes from these pages. Any insight that I have has ultimately been a gift from Him. May every word I ever write or speak be used for His purpose.

ABOUT THE AUTHOR

Davin Salvagno is the bestselling author of *Finding Purpose at Work*, the founder of PurposePoint, and the cofounder of The Purpose Summit and Heartcount™. He is a dynamic inspirational speaker known as one of the top voices on purpose and leadership in the world. His clients have included many Fortune 500 companies, universities, and Division I collegiate teams, and his work has been featured in *Forbes*, *Worth*, *Newsweek*, and the *Harvard Business Review*.

His breakthrough keynote talk, "The Power of Purpose," received international recognition in 2018, and his many talks since have helped hundreds of organizations across the world engage, inspire, and impact their people.

He is an honored member of the Marshall Goldsmith 100 Coaches, which recognizes the best coaches in the world, and a member of C12 Business Forums, a global peer advisory group comprised of more than four thousand Christian CEOs and business owners.

Davin is originally from Philadelphia, Pennsylvania, and now lives in Charlotte, North Carolina, with his wife, Amy, their two children, and their golden retriever, Brinkley.

For books, podcasts, and more resources, please visit DavinSalvagno.com.

Explore Davin's first book *Finding Purpose at Work.*

"As you read about Davin's twenty-year journey toward purpose, you'll become acquainted with the people and ideas that have shaped both his thinking on the power of purpose and his decision to share his passion with others. Davin's most sincere desire is to help you, the reader, realize the same satisfaction he has achieved as you do the work to discover your own purpose and that of your organization. Finding Purpose at Work is the blueprint that will guide you."

—Ken Blanchard, number one bestselling author of *The One Minute Manager*

Meet Davin at The Purpose Summit.

The Purpose Summit is one of the top transformative leadership experiences to attend for leaders who are passionate about creating people-focused and purpose-driven organizations. Learn more at ThePurposeSummit.com.

Book Davin to come speak to your organization.

Davin is represented by the Grey+Miller Agency, a leading speaking firm comprised of the world's most diverse, engaging, and influential speakers, authors, and thought leaders.

For speaking inquires please visit GrayMillerAgency.com or submit a request at BookDavin.com.

Mango Publishing, established in 2014, publishes an eclectic list of books by diverse authors—both new and established voices—on topics ranging from business, personal growth, women's empowerment, LGBTQ studies, health, and spirituality to history, popular culture, time management, decluttering, lifestyle, mental wellness, aging, and sustainable living. We were named 2019 and 2020's #1 fastest growing independent publisher by Publishers Weekly. Our success is driven by our main goal, which is to publish high-quality books that will entertain readers as well as make a positive difference in their lives.

Our readers are our most important resource; we value your input, suggestions, and ideas. We'd love to hear from you—after all, we are publishing books for you!

Please stay in touch with us and follow us at:

Facebook: Mango Publishing
Twitter: @MangoPublishing
Instagram: @MangoPublishing
LinkedIn: Mango Publishing
Pinterest: Mango Publishing
Newsletter: mangopublishinggroup.com/newsletter

Join us on Mango's journey to reinvent publishing, one book at a time.